GET
STARTED IN
WRITING
EROTIC
FICTION

Judith Watts and
Mirren Baxter

Teach ®
Yourself

Get Started in Writing Erotic Fiction

Judith Watts and
Mirren Baxter

First published in Great Britain in 2013 by Hodder & Stoughton. An Hachette UK company.

First published in the US in 2013 by The McGraw-Hill Companies, Inc.

Copyright © Judith Watts, Mirren Baxter 2013

The right of Judith Watts and Mirren Baxter to be identified as the Authors of the Work has been asserted by them in accordance with the Copyright, Designs and Patents Act 1988.

Database right Hodder & Stoughton (makers)

The Teach Yourself name is a registered trademark of Hachette UK.

British Library Cataloguing in Publication Data: a catalogue record for this title is available from the British Library.

Library of Congress Catalog Card Number: on file.

10 9 8 7 6 5 4 3 2 1

The publisher has used its best endeavours to ensure that any Website addresses referred to in this book are correct and active at the time of going to press. However, the publisher and the author have no responsibility for the Websites and can make no guarantee that a site will remain live or that the content will remain relevant, decent or appropriate.

The publisher has made every effort to mark as such all words which it believes to be trademarks. The publisher should also like to make it clear that the presence of a word in the book, whether marked or unmarked, in no way affects its legal status as a trademark.

Every reasonable effort has been made by the publisher to trace the copyright holders of material in this book. Any errors or omissions should be notified in writing to the publisher, who will endeavour to rectify the situation for any reprints and future editions.

Typeset by Cenveo® Publisher Services.

Printed and bound in Great Britain by CPI Group (UK) Ltd, Croydon CR0 4YY.

Hodder & Stoughton policy is to use papers that are natural, renewable and recyclable products and made from wood grown in sustainable forests. The logging and manufacturing processes are expected to conform to the environmental regulations of the country of origin.

Hodder & Stoughton Ltd

338 Euston Road

London NW1 3BH

www.hodder.co.uk

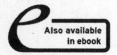

'The serpent beguiled me, and I did eat.'
Eve, Genesis 3:13

Acknowledgements

Thanks from Judith to:

- Phil Penman for not minding the research in bed, Beth for accepting my strange obsessions, Ruby for hiding the *Game of Thrones* DVDs, Eden for ignoring my open laptop
- my parents, for loving me anyway
- my friends, colleagues and students for expecting that I would finally write a book about writing about sex. You have all driven me on and have my passionate thanks.

Thanks from Mirren to:

- my lovely family, for giving me the space and the time, and for not seeming to mind at all
- MBM and GFM: my love to you both
- Fiona, Claire and Sue, willing guinea pigs, excellent writers and good friends
- my colleagues, who were surprised, and my friends, who weren't in the slightest.

Thanks from us both to:

- our wonderful contributors: Victoria Blisse, M.K. Elliot, Lucy Felthouse, Lily Harlem, Tabitha Rayne and Remittance Girl (Madeleine Morris)
- Laura Vile, who brought this project our way
- the team at Hodder, especially our editor, Victoria Roddam
- everyone at Eroticon 2013.

Contents

About the authors

We met while dropping our children off at primary school, and encouraged each other to write. Starting as beginners, we ended up with MFA degrees in Creative Writing, gaining adult teaching qualifications along the way. Together, we have over 30 years of experience in publishing, writing and helping others to achieve their creative goals. We've each spent many more years in bed with of all kinds of fictional characters.

Building on a previous career in traditional publishing, Judith is now Senior Lecturer in Publishing at Kingston University. Her academic interests include erotic literature, its history and sub-genres, and self-publishing. She is an editor and a published poet, performing erotic verse for unsuspecting audiences in suburban west London.

Working around her management career, Mirren taught creative writing in her local further education college. Now she works with small groups of writers as they complete and improve manuscripts prior to submission.

We are passionate about teaching, learning and passing on our skills. We understand that new writers often lack confidence; we've both been there. Devotees of erotic fiction, we're keen to see new talent and great writing coming on to the market.

Judith Watts and Mirren Baxter
www.hotjupiters.com

Introduction

This book is about writing about sex. We're saying this up front in case you've stumbled into it by accident. If straight talking about sex makes you uncomfortable, please stop reading now.

Bearing that in mind, we're going to ask you a question. It's the first of many. We'd like you to think about this question rather than letting your brain slide over it in the way that readers often do at the start of 'how-to' books. Here it is: What sexual fantasy works for you every single time?

Seriously. Think about your favourite fantasy, right now.

Did an image flicker across your mind, or a series of images? There's a good chance that, deep down in your dark insides, the very thought of that fantasy triggered a physical reaction. Humans are sexual beings with big brains. We think sexy thoughts and these thoughts affect our bodies. Our common humanity means that whatever turns you on is likely to turn on a lot of other people, too. And we just love stories. This is the premise behind erotic fiction.

When you pictured that image and felt that reaction, it's also likely that you managed to hide it; no one around you would have known what you were thinking or feeling. This lies behind the erotic fiction revolution. Online shopping and the e-reader changed the game. We didn't have to browse red-faced and conspicuous in the specialist section of the bookshop, reach for top-shelf titles, or brave the carefully neutral gaze of the shop assistant. Our private passion was indeed private. And with no blatant title or cover art on display, there was nothing to stop us enjoying other people's fantasies on the train, in the queue at the bank, or in the dentist's waiting room. No one could tell whether we were reading Austen or Nin. Those private passions could be indulged in public.

Then Fifty Shades of Grey by E.L. James went paper. It was everywhere, openly read and passed on to friends, to partners, to mothers and daughters. The previously uninitiated gorged themselves, and now we are all hungry. We want more stories with more sex and, frankly, we also want a bit of the authorial action. So, let's get started in writing erotic fiction.

First timers and improvers

Can anyone be a writer? If you can think in words, you can write. For complete beginners, we explain how fiction works and introduce you to the important aspects of our craft. Writing well about sex is difficult, even for experienced authors. We give you guidelines, the opportunity to practise, and we point out hazards along the way. Sustaining good writing for the length of a whole novel is a serious challenge. This book will help you to start small, but tells you how to handle longer stories when the time is right. And in these days of e-everything, it has never been easier to put your work in front of a potentially huge audience. We tell you about the various possible platforms for your own erotic fiction.

Women and men

Erotic fiction is read and written by both women and men. But we're not going to do the whole 'him/her' and '(s)he' thing in this book. It's too ugly. We will talk about 'you' and 'us', and if we have to get down to the third-person singular, we'll be using feminine constructions as often as it makes sense. We don't want men to feel left out, but you guys will have to just take it on the chin. Most published erotic fiction is written for and by women.

About this book

This book takes you from first inspiration, through writing your erotic fiction, to releasing your work.

The chapters have a practical outlook, with lessons, exercises and advice. You will find icons indicating several kinds of exercise, as follows.

Snapshot exercises are short and sweet. They ask you to carry out a simple and, hopefully, fun task such as coming up with a list of your sexual fantasies or likes.

 Workshop exercises are longer exercises that ask you to do a bit more work – for example working out the structure for a short story.

 Write exercises – self-explanatory – are the hardest but also, we hope, the most rewarding of the exercises.

 Edit exercises ask you to review, critique and improve your work.

Follow the chapters, complete the exercises, and your own erotic fiction will have reached an audience by the time you reach the end of the book. In addition, at the end of each chapter you will find focus points.

 Focus points will help you to hone in on the main ideas in each chapter as well as provide you with things to do to further your goal of becoming a writer of erotic fiction.

The Appendix includes further reading and lots of relevant websites. It's all here for you.

Finally, you need to bring your enthusiasm. And set up a special folder on your PC or buy a notebook just for your erotic fiction. Keep your work organized, because we often refer back to earlier exercises.

1

Erotic fiction

Whether you have decades of writing experience or you haven't written a creative word since leaving school, you can only ever start from where you are right now. This chapter is about looking at your starting point, and honouring what you think, believe and know.

Anyone with creative experience will tell you that the only certain way to improve is by practice. Musicians put in the hours to master scales and arpeggios so that their fingers automatically respond in performance. Writers need to practise putting actual words and punctuation together to bring their stories to life. While books like this can give you tools to speed up the process, real improvement will come only from making a mess on the page in the heat of a first draft, and then using revision techniques to tidy it all up.

Writers must actually write. So here's your first exercise.

The 'Big Sexy List'

Successful creative people are often asked where they get their ideas from. It's hard to answer this without sounding dismissive, because actively creative people know that ideas and inspiration can be found anywhere and everywhere – they are commonplace. The trick is to learn to recognize them when they come along, and to capture and store them so that they are available when you are reaching for something to write about.

Your Big Sexy List I

We're going to begin by capturing your ideas and inspirations relating to a very specific theme, gathering the material that will become the building blocks for your erotic fiction. If you only have a few minutes right now, that's fine. It's important to take action. Make a start. You can add to the list later.

- Make a list of everything that you think is sexy. The list can be bullet points, or even single words.
- Be precise in the details that you write down. Don't write 'cars' when you actually mean 'making out in the back seat of my boyfriend's Mini'. Getting the details right is a fundamental aspect of good writing, so practise it here.
- Keep writing until you stop coming up with ideas.
- Did you include the top fantasy that you thought about in the introduction?

This list is for your eyes only, but there may be some things that you'd be embarrassed to admit to in writing. Do not write these things down. There's a time and place for leaving your comfort zone and this is not it. We are just trying to collect material, not make you panic.

Here's a random selection of items from our lists:
- Whispering against lips
- Daniel Craig dressed only in a bath towel
- Sniffing the back of a neck
- That bit in *Shakespeare in Love* where he unwraps the bandages

- Petticoats
- The V muscle between abs and hip flexors.

If you're stuck, here are some prompts. Pick one and write until you've exhausted it, then pick another. Repeat until you run out of ideas.

- People – real-life or fictional
- Body parts and physical characteristics
- Scenes in books, films or television
- Music or songs
- Sexual acts or scenarios
- Items of clothing
- Other items
- Places
- Sensations.

Your Big Sexy List II

Look back over your list.

- Do you know why you find these particular things sexy?
- Are there stories behind any of the items? Or fantasies? Don't write these down just yet.
- Can you identify any themes?
- Are there any items on your list that surprise you?

We might have a few sexy elements in common, and we might have many broadly similar items. There might be things on our list that you find distinctly unsexy, and vice versa. What would the odds be that two people had exactly the same list? It's not going to happen. Your list is specific to your erotic imagination, and that's one of the things that makes your writer's voice unique. While it's true that probably everything that could be said about sex has already been said, no one's said it quite like you.

When you write erotic fiction, your own Big Sexy List will be a source of material. That's why we only wanted bullet points from you now, rather than developed stories. We want you to gather inspiration, not spend it.

Get into the habit of adding to your list as you notice what turns you on, or as you remember more things. Relax, then add to the list some more.

Reading erotic fiction

When we were growing up, porn wasn't readily available. We learned the basics of sex in the playground, we were taught about the anatomical bits and pieces from cross-section diagrams in biology classes, but we found out about the joy of it all from erotic fiction.

We had a lot of fun mapping our erotic fiction journeys.

JUDITH'S JOURNEY

- **Coming of age.** From Enid Blyton to *Scruples* by Judith Krantz (the rude bits, repeatedly). *The Story of O* in the local library, hot and bothered by whips and chains, fear of being caught. Later, shocked to discover it was written by a woman to her lover.
- **Late teens and early 20s.** Nancy Friday, *My Secret Garden*. Aha, not the only wicked girl whose sexual fantasies went against everything my feminist self believed in. Marquis de Sade – nasty but a bit turned on. Put right by reading Angela Carter's erotic reworking of fairy stories and the *Sleeping Beauty Trilogy* by Anne Rice writing as A.N. Roquelaure.
- **Late 20s onwards.** Anaïs Nin's *The Delta of Venus* and *Little Birds*, Henry Miller's *Tropic of Cancer*. Scarlet magazine, the Twilight series (for desire, anticipation and memories of first teen tingling). J.R. Ward and her band of Black Dagger Brothers, pressing the right buttons since 2005.
- **Now.** Anything and everything, especially on the bus. Erotic poetry. Waiting for someone to publish a *Venus in Furs* interactive story app to bring Sacher-Masoch's 1870 classic up to date.

MIRREN'S JOURNEY

- **Coming of age.** Battered Mills & Boon hand-me-downs, strange stirrings reading Judy Blume. William Bayer's *Punish Me with Kisses* introduced previously unimaginable things for grown-ups to do.
- **Late teens and early 20s.** Found boyfriend's porn stash. Gosh.
- **Late 20s onwards.** Felt sophisticated to be reading Nin, Miller and John Cleland's *Fanny Hill*. Fell in love with Edward Cullen.

- **Now.** Didn't fall in love with Christian Grey. Love my Kindle most of all. Always looking for something to fill the gaps between BDB releases.

Your reading history

Make a list of the significant moments in your own erotic fiction timeline.
- What books or stories did you enjoy the most?
- What did those narratives teach you about sex? Are you glad you found out this way?
- Has your taste in erotic fiction changed over time?
- Have you read enough to be able to write in this genre? If not, author suggestions in the Appendix may help. The best homework ever.
- Is there anything that you can add to your Big Sexy List?

If you've only recently decided that you'd like to write erotic fiction, you may feel like an impostor. This is common, even for writers with several publications under their belt. However, everything sexy that you've read and enjoyed in the past can be regarded as research, perhaps research that you could revisit and update. Your erotic fiction timeline is probably longer than you first thought.

Reading as a writer

Reading a story as a reader is significantly different from reading as a writer. For anyone who enjoys reading, it's not always easy to step away from the seductions of story and switch on your analytical brain. If you manage to disentangle yourself from the storyline, the books that you enjoy can be masterclasses in how to write well. The books you abandon can show you where writers get it wrong.

But you do need to go back to the page to see how it was done. It's likely that you'll be surprised by what you find there, because a lot of the story that you experienced will have come from your own imagination – you and the author are co-creators of your reading experience. We'll be talking more about this in Chapter 4.

In the meantime, try the following workshop exercise:

Analyse a hot scene

What's the most memorable sexy scene from your erotic fiction reading history? Seek it out and reread it. Don't get sucked into the rest of the story, just reread the one scene.

- Enjoy it, then define as precisely as you can what makes it is so hot. Is it possible to do this without referring to other scenes?
- If you own the book, underline words on the page, or rip it out and pin it up as a reminder of what hot writing looks like, as far as you are concerned.
- Copy it out word for word, getting the layout and the punctuation right. Pay attention to the language used and feel the rhythm of the sentences. Notice the moments that the author describes, and the gaps where she leaves you to fill in the details. Start to read like a writer.

 Lucy Felthouse, author

'Read as much as you possibly can in the genre. Not so you can try to emulate someone's writing, or rip off their ideas or characters, but so you can get an idea of how these stories work. How are they structured, what are the plots like, how is the sex scene executed? You'll also get an idea of how high the quality is of what's being published.'

Erotic fiction and porn

Some people just don't approve of sexual content in any form. They would say there is no difference between erotic fiction and written pornography, and that both are obscene.

Explicit sexual content is indeed the common factor between erotic fiction and porn, but they are not the same. They may at times have the same effect on the reader, but they go about it in different ways.

We're not going to delve into the politics of porn; that has been discussed at great length elsewhere. We're not anti-porn, but we're trying to pinpoint the differences between the two modes of writing to help you understand what you are getting into, and to give you some ammunition when you're challenged by someone who's uncomfortable with any sex on the page.

The new erotic fiction readers that bought *Fifty Shades of Grey* in their millions were not looking for porn. They wanted a sexy story.

Now, porn isn't known for its strong storylines. It's about the sexual act without any significant context. Sex is always on the cards, the characters are always up for it, and nothing gets in the way of their gratification. It is designed purely to arouse the reader.

Erotic fiction, on the other hand, wants to entertain the reader. It consists of stories about characters with their flaws, conflicts and complications, who have sex. The sex affects them and their lives. It messes with their emotions. Emotion is the key element in erotic fiction that's missing from porn. We identify with the characters and recognize their emotions, and that's what makes the sex interesting. Erotic fiction often derives much of its power from heightening emotion by ratcheting sexual tension; the characters have to wait for it. Desire rocks.

We don't think that any form of consensual sex is 'nasty', but we think that some porn and some erotic fiction can be. As readers, we want something better than that. We want sex to be meaningful for the characters, to let them discover more about their relationships or themselves. We're looking for mental as well as physical stimulation.

If romance draws a veil over sex, and porn gives us a close-up on the ins and outs, then erotic fiction is about what the characters experience. There's a place for all three types of writing. We like reading, and we think sex is a good thing. We want sex in our stories, and story with the sex.

No-go areas for published erotic fiction

All publishers draw a line between the subject matter that they will publish and that which they won't. Their boundaries define areas that are off-limits for legal or social reasons. General guidelines are:

- **All sexual acts should be legal and between consenting adults.** This means no children (no under-18s if you are considering the

American market, as 18 is the age of consent there), no incest, no animals, no forced sex, and no dead people unless they are the sexy undead, such as vampires.

- **No bodily functions,** namely watersports and scat (sexual activities involving urine and faeces). Readers might enjoy these kinks but retailers rarely carry them.
- **Nothing genuinely harmful or dangerous,** such as asphyxiation (breath control), and no life-destroying acts or scenarios.
- **No misery as the motivation for sex,** such as self-loathing, gender hatred or revenge. More joy is required.

It is impossible to give you hard-and-fast rules that apply to every imprint. You should always find and follow publishers' guidelines.

Varieties of erotic fiction

 ## Lily Harlem, author

'Erotic fiction and erotic romance are very much linked in my world. I don't often write pure erotica because sex without love is not my thing, though I have dabbled a few times and enjoyed the process and result. The romance, for me, is the emotion and the relationships behind the sex scenes. It doesn't have to be long-term love; it can be attraction, an obsession or even just the need for a one-night stand with an irresistible hottie.'

Erotic fiction publishers tend to market their books by sub-genre and theme. If you can categorize your writing according to publishers' criteria, your work is more likely to find the right audience.

To work within sub-genres and be accurately categorized, you must know and respect the conventions of the sub-genre. For example, an erotic romance usually ends with two individuals united in a committed relationship, at least for the time being. This ending is known as the Happily Ever After, or HEA.

Following conventions doesn't mean that stories are formulaic. In erotic fiction, we have some clear limits but, within those, we can give our imaginations and fantasies free rein. It's fun to work out the most interesting or subversive way to give the readers what they're looking for. And readers of genre fiction certainly do know what they want. Short-change the expectant reader at your peril.

The boundaries between different **sub-genres** of erotic fiction often blur. They change with shifts in cultural trends. At the time of writing, the community of readers, writers and publishers organizes the genre within a number of broad sub-genres:

- Classic or literary – the least likely to follow conventions, with more of a focus on writing style and characters, often involving a less optimistic storyline
- Contemporary – set in the contemporary world, with modern social values
- Erotic romance – essentially a love story with explicit sexual action
- Historical – medieval, Regency, gothic, steampunk, nineteenth and twentieth century
- Paranormal – fairy tales, fables and myths, shape-shifter, vampire, werewolf, ghost, angels, demons, gods and goddesses, urban fantasy
- Science fiction, futuristic and time travel
- Mystery, thriller, suspense and crime
- Horror
- Comedy
- Action and adventure
- Western, cowboys, or Bollywood – culture-specific settings, characters and issues

Any genre can be given an erotic twist. Sub-genres of erotic fiction are closely related to their non-erotic counterparts – erotic science fiction uses conventions popular in mainstream science fiction.

If your work is adding sexual content to a mainstream genre, you should find out that genre's conventions, too. An erotic thriller will benefit from the same plotting tips and characterization techniques as a regular thriller.

There's a lot to get right. This will be easier if you've read widely in your chosen sub-genre. If you're building a fantasy world, the reader needs to know the rules of that world. If it's historical erotica, you need to recreate and sustain the period in detail. If your story is culture- or location-specific, do your research and look at other writers who represent that culture well. Mystery or suspense needs to be plot driven and wrought with tension that's not just sexual. If you want to write sci-fi, look at how the specialists do it.

An equally broad range of **sexual themes** are found within the erotic fiction categories. This list is not exhaustive, but here are the major themes in current erotic fiction:

- BDSM – stories with a strong bondage/domination/sadism/masochism element
- Age-related – May to December, cougar, sugar daddy, silver fox and twenties
- Unconventional sexuality, such as captive, kink and fetish
- Gender and sexuality-related themes, such as lesbian, gay, bisexual, transgender, queer, questioning and intersex, covering characters and lifestyles from the whole spectrum (titles can be listed on publishers' sites as, for example, LGBT, M/M or F/F)
- Dark erotica – sexual fantasy taken to dark and disturbing places (being forced, complete loss of power, consent twisted out of shape)
- Interracial and multicultural
- *Ménage* and polyamory – multiple partners, from threesomes up
- Specific place and time related, such as holiday or Christmas collections
- Rubenesque, plus-size, or curve appeal.

Many publishers don't separate out sub-genres and themes like this – their lists contain a mixture of both. We've separated them to help you understand that erotic fiction combines the type of book and the type of sex. Pick a combination you like.

Whatever your gender or sexual identity, if you're writing from a position that's not your own, you'll need to work hard to give your characters credibility in their relationships.

Technology enables readers to search specifically for the thing that turns them on. The Ellora's Cave site aims to provide state-of-the-art searchability – whatever readers are in the mood for, they can find. For example, if your current taste is for an erotic romance e-book that's set in the future and features a male–male interracial couple – oh, and a special offer would be good – then you should be able to find it with just a few keystrokes.

Some erotic fiction publishers have borrowed a business model that's familiar from the romance genre – the 'category' title. A category romance is around 55,000 words long, and the stories meet clearly defined criteria. Several books are issued every month in each line. Erotic fiction's category conventions are less prescriptive than those for romantic fiction, but publishers' guidelines for submission and recommendations about sexual content ensure that category books meet readers' specific requirements.

Lily Harlem, author

'If you can find a sub-genre that hits your buttons as you write and then gets readers snapping up your book, then stick with it!'

Heat ratings

'Heat rating' systems are unique to erotic fiction.

When books were banned because of sexual content, the limits of morality were set by the legal system. Today, when almost anything goes, erotic fiction titles are not subject to the same statutory classifications and regulations as those found in the film and gaming industries. However, some publishers have adopted a similar descriptive method.

Erotic heat ratings are somewhat subjective – one person's fiery pit is another's candle flame. Yet there seems to be a general consensus as to levels of ignition:

- **Sensual.** For a mainstream audience, this simmers sweetly on a low heat, with conventional sex and words that provide a hint of spice.
- **Steamy.** Still for a general audience, this is a more heightened erotic experience, with lots of sexual tension, adult language and graphic details.
- **Sizzling or squirming.** Moving away from the mainstream, this fiction enters the explicit, experimental and imaginative end of the spectrum.
- **Scorching or burning.** Uninhibited, these titles are even more imaginative, with unconventional sex, language and encounters.

- **Extremely hot or blazing out of control.** Risqué plots with hard-core scenes and language. No-holds-barred, anything goes. Not for the faint-hearted. Stories with this level of heat may move into areas that are considered taboo and push the genre to its limits.

Ratings applied by different publishers can be found on their websites. Take a look at Siren and Total-E-Bound for examples. Total-E-Bound has a sexometer to indicate how much sex is in a book, where level 1 has mostly erotic tension with a sex scene finale, level 2 balances tension and sex, and level 3 has sexual interaction throughout.

Writing to meet conventions and within rating systems ensures that readers don't have a nasty shock.

There's more detail in the Appendix about the most popular sub-genres and themes. We also provide a sample list of authors and anthologies.

Crossing the line

Published erotic fiction will generally follow the no-go guidelines we mentioned earlier, but certain categories of fiction may offer exceptions:

- **Sexual behaviour and fantasies.** A mixture of fiction and non-fiction, the stories in collections such as Nancy Friday's *My Secret Garden* include elements that cross the line. Reported fantasies include underage sexuality and bestiality.
- **Erotic classics.** Anaïs Nin breached the rules of legality and consent. She sometimes neglected character development, and she didn't make them wait for gratification. But her stories are classics of erotic fiction rather than pornography because she writes beautifully. De Sade is still the poster boy for scat a cool 200 years after his death, possibly because he has little competition.
- **Dubious consent and non-consensual sex (dub-con and non-con).** Publishers of erotic fiction generally require 'safe, sane and consensual' sex scenes. The market no longer tolerates bodice-ripper stories about women being taken against their will. In real life, sex without consent is rape, but the boundaries of consent are sometimes blurred in fiction. For example, in paranormal

erotic fiction, a vampire compels a human to have sex. This is non-consensual. In dark erotica, a kidnapper forces sex on his victim. If the victim welcomes the sexual contact, and if the writer has handled it well, some level of consent is implied. This is dubious consent. Consent role play, rough play and power play all involve characters giving each other permission to act out their non-consensual fantasies.

- **Coming of age.** We can all relate to the thrill of first fumblings and desire. Publishers are picking up on the trend for 'steamies', dubbed in the US 'Judy Blume for the *Fifty Shades* generation'. These are escapist romances with emotional connections and passion rather than graphic sex. *Irresistible* by Liz Bankes is a good example. There are ongoing debates about age-appropriate content for the Young Adult (YA) market and reading censorship. Writers in this market must accept that they have responsibilities to their readers. As well as a demanding audience, writers face intermediaries such as parents, librarians and teachers. This is a sub-genre of YA publishing, not erotic fiction.

You may recognize some of these no-go areas from your reading.

Going no-go

Can you identify something on the no-go list that you might like to explore in writing one day? If you haven't added this to your Big Sexy List, consider doing that now. When you are ready to stretch the boundaries, this might be a place to start.

Philosophy

With the Big Sexy List exercise at the start of this chapter, you thought about the triggers for your own erotic response, the sex that you explore in your own head. It's also important to think about what you intend to say to the outside world.

Sex is an emotive subject. It continues to be the subject of moral, legal and political debate. By writing and sharing erotic fiction, you become an active participant in that debate. Before you make a statement, it's a good idea to be clear about your own position. You need to know what you're trying to say.

After many years of thinking about sex, here's what we believe.

- Sex can be a lot of fun.
- We defend anyone's right to enjoy their own sexuality to the full, as long as they are not harming anyone else.
- We defend anyone's right to do what they want with their own body.
- Some people will strongly identify themselves as asexual, homosexual, bisexual or heterosexual, but others will have a more fluid sexual self-image. It's all good as far as we are concerned.
- Everyone has their own limits when it comes to sex. As we read and write, we can explore the extent of those limits. Part of the thrill of erotic fiction is the glimpse into someone else's sexual adventures, characters finding themselves in the borderlands of their own sexuality, testing their limits. And those characters brave enough to transgress, to cross the line, seem to have the most fun.

Our philosophical position is reflected in the Sex Positive movement. If you'd like to find out more about this, there are many resources on the Internet.

 ## What do you think?

Take some time to pinpoint exactly what you think about sex and sexuality. If you think that sex should only be part of a loving, committed heterosexual relationship, you will probably want to focus on erotic romance. If you think that marriage is a form of social control, you probably won't be championing the HEA.

Health and safety

There are some pitfalls when writing about a sexual act that you have not experienced yourself. You should know what the standard safe practice is for any act, and make sure your characters follow that practice. While some people just read for the thrill and the warm fuzzy feeling, others will want to try the fictitious scenarios that have turned them on. You certainly don't want to be responsible for causing your reader any harm, so make sure they are informed.

In saying that, we're in the business of entertainment, not education. If your character is the kind that would use a condom, have him use it. If not, don't force it into the scene. For example, although dental dams have a recognized place in safe sex, they're exceptionally rare in the genre.

For all the harm that can be caused by unsafe sexual practices, we don't think that readers are harmed by reading erotic fiction. Some readers might find certain sexual acts disgusting. This might stop them reading, or they might read on to try to understand, or they might find themselves aroused even though they are disgusted. This can lead to an expansion of sexual self-awareness. Erotic fiction can show readers that they're not alone with a sexual reaction that perplexes them.

Tabitha Rayne, author

'I love erotica. There is so much to explore within the sub-genres – you can read and write about absolutely anything. Sex and the sexual/spiritual connection between my characters are always the most important element within my books. However, it is the plot and story journey that facilitate this. I feel my true voice comes from within the genre but my story-telling encompasses so many themes, from paranormal, historical to romance and dystopian fantasy – how many other genres can do all that?'

Focus points

We hope that this introduction to the genre has started you thinking about your place within it. Here are some things to remember and some things to do as you progress through this book and into your erotic fiction career.

Things to remember

- You don't have to step out of your own comfort zone until you're ready.
- Porn is about sex. Erotic fiction is about characters, emotions, consequences and sex.
- Publishers are looking for erotic fiction that is positive and life-affirming and which depicts only legal scenarios.

Things to do

- Pay attention to the things that turn you on. Make a note of them because they will inspire your writing.
- Read like a writer – go back to the page and work out how it's done.
- There are many sub-genres of erotic fiction. Identify which section of the market you're drawn to and make this your focus. Read widely from it and learn the conventions.
- Know your own philosophy about sex and about writing about sex. Make creative choices that support your philosophy.

Where to next?

In Chapter 2 we'll be introducing some of the tips and tricks that will turn you from a self-aware reader into a happy and productive writer. And we'll have a go at writing some sexy stuff, too.

2

Becoming a writer

If all the writers in the world waited for the muse to move them before they started to write, there would be very little for the rest of humanity to read. Other things get in the way of creative intentions if we let them – the day job, food shopping, haircut, algebra homework, crap TV. This chapter is about the steps that you can take in your day-to-day life to support your dream of becoming a writer.

In the Big Sexy List, you took erotic inspirations out of your head and put them on the page. Ideas on the page can be stored and remembered, they can be examined and worked on and moulded to the shape that best suits your creative needs. So, because you need to write regardless of whether you feel inspired or not, and because you must get things on to the page so that you can do something with them, here's your first writing exercise:

'The First Time'

First times carry significant weight. Whether it's the first meeting, the first kiss or your first publication, these occasions often involve strong and varied emotions, ranging from nervous trepidation to delirious excitement. They are fun to write about and satisfying to read.

- Write about the first time. Which first is up to you, but make it sexual, important and positive.
- Start with 'It all happened when ...'
- Just write. Include everything you want to say about that memorable first. Don't worry about spelling or grammar. Enjoy remembering. Aim for 500 words.

Reflect on the process

Instead of looking at what you've put on the page, think about the process of writing.

- From 0 (unfeasibly simple) to 10 (requiring blood, sweat and tears), how difficult did you find the writing?
- Can you identify what made it so easy or so difficult?
- What can you do to make things easier the next time you write? If you don't know yet, we're going to cover some key factors in this chapter.
- What have you learned about writing by doing that one exercise? There will definitely be something, whether it's how long it takes to write a page of prose, how much you hate writing with pencil, or an innovative solution to the perennial 'show, don't tell' problem (more on that later). Identify and note down what you've learned.

When you've finished writing, put your manuscript away for a while. The best time to revise your work is when you've partly forgotten what you have written. But keep it safe. We'll ask you to look out your version of 'The First Time' in later chapters.

Tabitha Rayne, writer

'If you want to write good erotica, write stories that turn you on. That's it!'

First-time writers

Exactly the same skills are needed for writing erotic fiction as for any other kind of fiction. On the plus side, erotic fiction can be a lot more fun to write than other genres. On the downside, sex is the only literary theme that we know of that has its own internationally reported award for writers who do it badly. That's because many writers do do it badly.

First-time writers often identify three worries:

1 'I don't know where to start.'

2 'I don't know if my idea is any good.'

3 'I wrote something but, when I read it, it was really bad.'

It's good news when a writer raises these problems; she's aware of her current limitations and this self-awareness is critical if she wants to improve. These three worries relate to the sets of skills that all writers need to be able to call upon, skills that are often lumped together under the heading 'writing'.

Writing skill sets

- **Skill Set 1: Creativity** – knowing where to start
  - Generating and capturing ideas
  - Setting goals
  - Getting down to work

- **Skill Set 2: Storytelling** – developing good ideas
  - Understanding audience expectations
  - Building strong storylines
  - Creating characters, settings and story events
- **Skill Set 3: Word craft** – writing well
  - Using the right words
  - Making the story real for the reader
  - Keeping the reader in the story

There's a progression through these skill sets. Everyone engaged in a creative work needs Skill Set 1. Anyone dealing with story, such as film-makers, choreographers and writers, needs Skill Set 2. All writers need Skill Set 3.

Most writers don't consciously break down their talent into these skill sets, juggling all the elements as needed. That's fine as long as things are going well but, if you encounter any difficulties in getting your creative vision on to the page, it helps if you can define the areas that you need to work on.

By the end of this book, you'll have been introduced to and practised all of these skills:

- For **Skill Set 1**, the exercises in Chapter 1 about the Big Sexy List and looking back on your reading of erotic fiction were designed to help your creativity, by starting to capture ideas. We'll talk some more about this in Chapter 3 – Research. The rest of this current chapter will cover setting goals and getting down to work.
- We started to look at **Skill Set 2** in relation to what readers expect from the sub-genres and heat levels. There's more in Chapters 4 to 6, about storytelling, character and plot.
- We will look at **Skill Set 3** in Chapters 7 to 9, covering writing well, writing about sex and revision.

New writers' worries can also plague experienced, published and hugely successful writers. They may doubt the quality of their ideas and their writing. But experienced writers know to keep writing. They power on through their doubts, either dispelling them or identifying the root cause of the problem and fixing it if it can be fixed, or ditching it if it can't. Experienced writers have the further advantage that they know where to start. The only way to become a more experienced writer? You already know the answer to that one, but see the rest of this chapter for ways to go about it.

Your writing dreams

There may be lots that you've still to learn about writing. Why do you bother? It's time to think big:

- What are your wildest dreams for your erotic fiction?
- Where would you ideally stand between writing strictly for your eyes only and global domination?
- What might stop you achieving your dreams?

Setting goals

Wildest dreams can come true but it usually takes hard work and good luck. As Samuel Goldwyn said, the harder we work, the luckier we get. So, it's time to identify the things you'll need to do to prepare yourself and get those dreams within your reach.

Why set goals? In life, we sometimes realize that we want to be somewhere else and we need a plan to get there. Goals are about things that you can take action on to bring yourself closer to that desired somewhere else. Dreams, on the other hand, often relate to outcomes rather than actions, things that are not always within your control. While it's good to dream, solid goals are at the heart of achievement.

The short story goal

Erotic fiction has a thriving short story market. It's possibly the healthiest short story market around. The literary short story is often regarded as difficult to master. However, we recommend that anyone starting to write erotic fiction begins by writing short stories. This is for three reasons:

1 You need broadly the same skills to write short and long fiction, so the short story is a good place to learn and practise.

2 There is less chance of your enthusiasm for your story running out before you complete it.

3 **With the thriving market, you have more of a chance of finding an audience.**

If you work through the exercises in this book, you will have at least one short story out there in the world by the time you reach the end. Your wildest dreams may be more ambitious than delivering one short story, but getting your first story out is an important short-term goal.

 ## M.K. Elliott, author

'The short story is underrated. When it's good, it's really good. A short story can pull you into its world within the first few lines, thrust you through intense drama and then surprise you at the end. Writing erotic short stories is sometimes even harder than writing non-erotic stories. Of course, the sex is important. It has to be smoking hot and it needs to happen within a few pages. However, this doesn't mean that the story itself should be lost, or that the characters have any less depth or background.'

Short stories often come in at around 5,000 to 7,000 words, which equates to approximately 25 pages in a printed book. Writers and publishers rarely talk about numbers of pages, because this depends on many things such as the size of the page and margins, the spacing and font. We always use word count for an accurate measure of how much work has been done, and how much is still to be done. This book is about 72,500 words long. From now on, you should think in word count. Six thousand words or so of a standard-length short story can seem very long indeed if you haven't written much before. Don't worry – we'll build up to it.

How long you'll take to finish this book depends on how fast you read, how hard you're willing and able to work, how deeply you go into the additional reading, and how many other distractions you'll be facing in the coming weeks. In our experience, it is difficult to get anything creative done if it doesn't come with a deadline attached. It's also difficult to honour a completely self-generated deadline. (Some marvellous external deadlines can be found if you look out for calls for submission.)

If we suggest you should have finished this book, completed a short story and sent it out on its way two months from today, does that seem reasonable? If it's not reasonable, what would be a realistic deadline?

Your goals

Short-term goals are the things you commit to achieving in one year:

- What is your standard year? We're used to working with academic years.
- What do you commit to achieving in your writing by the end of this year? If you feel too close to that date, think about next year.
- What are the three most important goals, the ones that will move you towards those wild dreams? Put them in order from top priority down.
- Set specific deadline dates for achieving these goals.
- Have you included the goal of getting your first short story out into the erotic fiction community? If not, what are you including in its place?

Look at your top-priority short-term goal:

- What must you do to achieve that goal? Can you identify each action you need to take, and put the actions in the right order?
- When can you realistically expect to have completed each action? Put dates against them. Do the same for each of your short-term goals.
- Look at your calendar and commitments. Are your action dates achievable in the context of the rest of your life? Have you been too easy on yourself? Or too ambitious? Adjust dates as needed.

Longer-term goals are also worth thinking about:

- What do you want to achieve, in life and in writing, within the next ten years?
- Where do you need to be in five years' time to be at that point in ten years? Where do you need to be in two years to hit that five-year target?
- What about one year?
- How does this one-year achievement relate to your short-term goals? Do you need to change them? Or do you need to change your two-year timetable?

If you feel that you don't know enough about writing to set strong goals, don't worry – they're not written in stone. As you work through this book, you'll learn more and you'll be able to refine your targets and dates. Setting goals is a planning process. When they're put into action, plans often change.

Getting down to work

- Identify some time every day for your writing. As a minimum, everyone can find 15 minutes a day for their highest-priority short-term goal. Beyond those 15 minutes, you'll be thinking about your story a lot more. So, those 15 minutes of actual words-on-page are the tip of your creative iceberg.
- If you have more time, keep writing. However, there's a point where your word count dwindles. Stop before you reach that point – you have better things to do with your time. Try dividing your time into 30-minute chunks – 25 minutes of writing and a 5-minute break.
- Faced with a huge expanse of time, it's easy to waste it. Good work often gets done when there are constraints, when there's not a second to waste. Can you write in your lunch hour, or for 15 minutes before that appointment?
- Does your writing flow better at a particular time of the day? Try getting up early to write, or staying up late.
- In the early stages, you might be spending more time researching than writing. But remind yourself to actually write for at least 15 minutes every day.
- You will want to skip days. Resist this.
- If there is a day when you genuinely can't write, make sure that you find time to research, or plan or revise your work. Keep your project in the forefront of your mind. If you can't even find time for that, do what you have to do, then get back to the writing the next day.
- Is there something you can give up to create writing time?

Writing 15 words per minute is an achievable target – this sentence is 15 words long. Multiply that by 15 minutes, and you reach 225 words per day. Writing every day, you'll complete a 6,000-word short story in 27 days. You can certainly do that. If you do that for a year, you'll have 13 short stories under your belt, and your writing will have improved dramatically. And if you're writing every day, it gets easier and faster. You could double your word count.

You could write a novel in 15-minute chunks, if that's all the time you have.

If you're stuck for something to write about, pick one of the items on your Big Sexy List, and write about that.

Keep a journal. In it, you can reflect on your progress and record the thing that you've learned or confirmed on that day, about your writing practice, your technique or your story. Read through these insights and remind yourself of the lessons you've learned.

The writing habit

The key task for the new writer is to get into the daily writing habit.

Think about a time when you deliberately took on a new habit. It might be making changes to your diet, or exercising, or even stopping an old habit, such as smoking, and replacing it with something else. Was it easy to change your habit? What helped you to make the change? What setbacks did you face, and how did you deal with them?

We are challenging you to form a new habit, daily writing, by writing for 15 minutes every day for a month.

Making a habit of it

- **Make a plan.** Do you need to clear time for writing? Pick a start date and gear up. Plan what you're going to write. Understand how this month of writing will help you achieve your short- and long-term goals.

- **Make it easy.** Keep your materials and equipment organized and stored in the right place. If you have write in different places, organize everything into a bag so that you're ready to go. Keep supplies to hand and batteries charged. Don't try to change anything else in your life at the same time; just concentrate on your writing habit for a month. You might want to tie this habit to a specific trigger, for example that you always write first thing in the morning, as soon as you wake up.

- **Get support.** Let your nearest and dearest know what you are doing for this month and make sure they know not to disturb you – they'll have to learn new habits, too. Join a writing circle or get on to a discussion forum.
- **Stay positive.** Remember that new writers often think that their work is no good. Trust the process. Show up every day and do the work.
- **Keep a record.** Get a calendar, put a big tick on every day that you write, and aim for every day to have a tick. Identify what you have learned or confirmed for that day and write it in your journal. How many words did you do? Make a note.
- **Be kind to yourself.** Sometimes the outside world intervenes. If you end up missing a day, remember the big picture and your long-term plans – one day is not going to make that much difference.

The writing habit can be a way of dealing with the dreaded writer's block. If you do 15 minutes every day, it doesn't need to be on your big project, the one that's causing you all the anxiety. It can be a less threatening piece based on a prompt. Keep the words coming, keep your writing muscles limber, and keep yourself ready for the day when you're back in control of your bigger work.

Focus points

In this chapter we've started you writing. We've introduced the writing skill sets to give you context for the topics that we'll cover later in this book.

Things to remember

- Beginning writers struggle with knowing where to start, assessing their ideas, and hating their own work. You will learn how to handle these problems with experience.
- Writers need creative, storytelling and word-craft skills. Again, these come with experience.
- To gain experience, you need to write.
- You can write any length of fiction in 15 minutes a day if that's all the time you have.
- By trial and error, you will find the best place, time and tools for your writing.

Things to do

- Write every day.
- Commit to getting a short story out there two months from now, or pick a reasonable timescale.
- Plan your writing future by setting long- and short-term goals, identifying actions to be taken, and setting deadlines for those actions.
- After every writing session, make a note of what to have learned or confirmed.
- Make daily writing your new habit, and work on embedding this habit for the coming month and beyond.
- **Write every day!** We really mean it.

Where to next?

In Chapter 3 – Research – we will discover the joys of finding out more about sex, and we'll think about some potential pitfalls.

3

Research

When we carry out research for our writing, we're looking for three things:

1 Inspiration. When you find out about something new and put it together with something you're already interested in, creative sparks fly. So if you want to write about oral sex and you stumble across some really cool information about hot-air ballooning, you suddenly have an interesting setting and, along with that, some new sensations for your characters.

2 Structure. It often helps to have an external process that you can use to define the stages and limits of your story. For example, what are the stages of a half-hour hot-air balloon flight? Do certain things always happen at certain times? How much time does that leave for the blow job?

3 Credibility. You need to get things right, or you'll lose credibility with readers. You must write convincingly about hot-air ballooning. What technical terms are used? What does it really feel like? What are the rules that are always followed?

Of course, your research could as easily be about the sexual act as the hot-air ballooning.

There are a few downsides to carrying out research for your writing:

1 **Over-enthusiastic research. Don't get lost in it all. If you've got an enquiring mind and access to the Internet, it's too easy to lose days on end reading up about really cool stuff. You're not trying to write a dissertation about hot-air ballooning. Or oral sex, for that matter. What's more, the tantalizing detail that you are holding out for may not exist.**

2 **Under-enthusiastic note taking. It's incredibly frustrating to look back at your research notes (you are keeping notes, aren't you?) and find that you haven't recorded a particular detail clearly enough, then realizing that you also haven't noted the source. Be consistent in recording the date and sources for all your research, even if that source is yourself.**

3 **Over-enthusiastic writing. Too much technical information will kill the story dead. You probably don't need to include everything you've found out about hot-air balloons – it will bore the average reader.**

With all of that in mind, this chapter is about some key places to look for the additional information you need for your erotic fiction.

Memories

We've already looked at some of your erotic memories. 'The First Time' exercise was explicitly about memory, as was the exercise about your reading history. This section of the book is exercise-heavy. That's because, as we've mentioned before, you can't work with things that are only in your head.

WRITE WHAT YOU KNOW?

There's an ancient debate about the idea that, as a writer, you should 'write what you know'. We think that experience is the foundation for any writing. But it's only the foundation. You know what it feels like to really want someone, or to be nervous about trying something new, or to have that first kiss. In reading erotic fiction, the story is effective and affective because the reader can tap into her own memories of what it's like for *that* to happen, or the closest thing to it that she's experienced.

Erotic memory

You're going to write about something that has happened to you in real life. Pick one of these topics:

- A time when you wanted to have sex, but you didn't because of external reasons, such as no privacy or no contraception.
- A time when you did something sexual that you'd never done before.
- A time when you became aware of other people having sex.

Before you start writing, close your eyes and think carefully about that time. Remember what the surroundings were like and who you were with. Think in terms of your five senses – what could you see, feel, smell, taste, touch? Was anything said? What were you thinking about the things that were happening? Run through the events in your mind a few times.

Decide whether you're going to write from your own point of view, using 'I', or as though you were a different character, using 'she' or 'he'.

Now, write. Don't worry about the following:

- writing well
- making mistakes with spelling, punctuation or grammar
- getting it wrong (you can't – it's your story).

But do write proper text – don't just make notes.

Aim for at least 1,000 words.

The following exercise is important for two reasons. First of all, sexual experiences prompt a complex range of emotions. Second of all, you know what emotions feel like. You can call upon your own experiences and use them to add credible detail to your erotic fiction, to help the reader feel the truth of your characters' experiences.

Emotional memory

One of the main differences between erotic fiction and porn is that erotic fiction deals with the characters' emotions. Here's some memory-based research you can do on emotions.

1   Make a list of as many emotions as you can. Brainstorm and grow your list – it will be a resource for future reference. Don't worry about whether something is an emotion or a feeling – they all work for our purposes.

2   Pick one of them, but not love, lust or hate.

3   What is your own strongest memory of that emotion? Think deeply about that occasion. This might be difficult for you. If it's too difficult at the moment, pick another, less threatening emotion. Remember that you don't have to leave your comfort zone until you are ready.

4   Write about the occasion that prompted that strong emotion. You can write either in note form or in full text – whatever feels most comfortable. Include all the information that you can remember about what happened, how it started, how it felt, how things progressed, how you felt afterwards. Include sensory details – what you saw, heard, felt (as in touched), smelled, tasted. Search your memory. Make sure that you are using language that is as truthful and precise as possible.

5   If you haven't written about the emotion in relation to a sexual situation, how could that emotion come into play in sexual scenarios?

6   Look at your notes. Circle the words or phrases that you've used that might be useful in a piece of erotic fiction and note them in your journal.

7   You may find that your memory has sparked a story idea, or that you can so easily imagine an erotic scenario that you are keen to write it. Great – go for it.

8   Repeat the process for other emotions as the opportunity or need arises.

Sexual memory

- How much do you know about sex?
- Have you had a variety of sexual experiences, or many experiences of the same flavour?
- Which specific sexual experiences make your top five? Write them down. Is there a common theme?
- Pick your all-time number one. Try to define exactly what made that experience so very good. Was it to do with intensity, experimentation, or transgression? What emotions did you feel?
- Write about that experience, in note form or in full text. As with the emotional memory exercise, include all the information that you can remember about what happened, how it started, how it felt, how things progressed, how you felt afterwards. Include sensory details – what you saw, heard, felt (touched), smelled, tasted. Use truthful and precise language.
- Make a list of all the different sexual things you've done. Did you like them? How much? If there's anything you didn't enjoy, is there any way that, if things were different, you might have enjoyed it more? For example, what if your partner had been more confident?
- Is there anything positive in the bad sex you've had? Is there anything comic in the good or bad sex?
- Which sexual activities do you wish you'd experienced? Did you ever get close to trying them? What stopped you? What have you done that's similar, or almost-but-not-quite that experience?

It's likely that you already know a lot. Your reading of the different categories of erotic fiction will tell you whether you know enough to write in them. If you think your experience is limited, the last question raises another possibility – write your fantasies. You can get pretty far with bit of extrapolation from what you already know and a fevered imagination. You don't have to be part of the dogging scene to write about it. Track down a TV documentary for the logistics, and your imagination will fill in the blanks. Although, if you've always wanted to try it, now you have the perfect excuse.

Erotic fiction is fundamentally about fantasy. This includes trying things out to see if you like them, and then trying them some more if you want. All of this experimentation occurs in a place of safety – on the page. If you're not willing to take the risks involved in gaining direct experience, you need to make sure that your other research is spot on, and that includes carefully mining your memories and exploring your fantasies.

THE PROBLEM WITH MEMORIES

Real life does not always make credible stories. For example, the outrageous coincidences that can happen in reality are not suited to fiction. In fiction, plot events – the things that happen – must serve the needs of the story. It's more important to write a coherent narrative than to include everything that happened. It's erotic *fiction*. If someone criticizes your story choices, you cannot legitimately defend your art by saying 'but that's what really happened'. Chapter 6 is all about structuring stories.

Experts

Is your own experience patchy? Is your imagination unable to supply all the details that you need to write with authority? It's time to call in the experts. An expert has the knowledge that you lack, and her knowledge is usually recognized within her field. While you're looking for facts to bolster your credibility, it's likely that you will stumble across juicy titbits that boost your inspiration levels, either in relation to your current project or for future use. And it's a real thrill when a well-formed structure unexpectedly lands in your lap.

In what follows, we talk a lot about using the Internet as a resource. However, it can be astonishingly easy to get out of your depth online. If you're going to access adult sites, use a trusted portal. For example, the excellent Jane's Guide (janesguide.com) is a curatorial service, commenting on sex-related websites, informing readers about what they're likely to find before they make that click. The Erotic Readers & Writers Association (ERWA) website is another helpful gateway.

Lucy Felthouse, author

'In this Internet age, we're incredibly lucky when it comes to research. You can find out all kinds of things without even getting out of your chair. Of course, you have to be careful that your sources are genuine and correct – it's always worth double-checking if you're not sure. Some sub-genres of erotica and erotic romance need more research than others. In historical, for example, your facts must be absolutely correct. Other sub-genres, of course, need none. You can make up new worlds and creatures of your own and nobody can say you're wrong.'

NON-FICTION

We do love a good 'how-to' book. Most readers are aware of the *Kama Sutra*, which is more poetic than practical, and *The Joy of Sex*, which leans the other way. However, there are hundreds, if not thousands, of modern manuals that explain the how-to and how-not-to of sexual practices. The ones worth reading are those that include information on keeping yourself and your partner safe.

Nancy Friday's *My Secret Garden* was first published in 1973. A collection of sexual fantasies contributed by anonymous women, it offered reassurance to the reader that she wasn't alone in her particular brand of kink. It's perhaps dated now, reflecting its time in some of the details and the women's concerns. But, as a research resource, along with her later books on developments in female fantasy and on male fantasy, it includes a breadth of sexual taste that may extend your horizons. *My Secret Garden* is less provocative than many modern books, but it is fondly regarded as a new classic. Emily Dubberley produced a modern update in 2013 with *Garden of Desires: The Evolution of Women's Sexual Fantasies*.

Published in 2002, *The Encyclopaedia of Unusual Sex Practices*, edited by Brenda Love (really!), is a good way to learn more, all delivered in a rather matter-of-fact and clinical style. We challenge you to read the glossary without laughing and, more importantly, learning a thing or two. It's a good source of basic inspiration and you can let your imagination loose from there.

Non-fiction sex bloggers don't just kiss and tell. As well as providing regular updates on their real-life sexual experiences, the best of them cover sexual education, political and social comment, product and book reviews, and links to other relevant websites and blogs. You might like to take a look at the blog by Violet Blue, an American writer with a lot to say from a very professional and stylish platform, and Dirty Little Whispers, a lively sex blog from the UK. Good sex blogs are explicit without being sleazy.

Sex memoir successes include *The Intimate Adventures of a London Call Girl* by Belle de Jour, and *Girl with a One-track Mind* by Abby Lee. Sex memoirs are often criticized as being fictionally enhanced accounts of real life. We don't think that's too much of a problem, to be honest, as long as you are aware that there may have been some polishing of the narrative.

Lots of men and women watch porn. We're not saying that porn films are non-fiction, and their 'storylines' aren't right for erotic fiction. But porn is a rich source of factual visual information, particularly in relation to sex positions, to what's physically possible, and to what faces, gestures and bodies look like during sex. It can take you from nought to 60 on a previously unheard-of kink in a very short space of time. There have been changes in some branches of pornography over recent years, including initiatives offering explicit sexual content created for and by women. There's also an interesting move towards 'real sex' porn. Again, be careful if you go looking for porn on the Web.

OTHER STORIES

Other stories are rich sources of material for sexual fantasies. Source material – whether it's in a book, a film or a television programme – doesn't have to be the slightest bit provocative. The engaged reader's imagination embellishes the relationships between characters, as witnessed by the amount of slash fan fiction on the Web. ('Slash fanfic' involves taking another writer's characters and creating explicit and often gay sexual scenarios for them – think Dr Who and a cyberman, Mr Darcy and Mr Rochester, or Lara Croft and Brangelina.) As a writer, fiction is best viewed as a source of inspiration rather than hard factual detail. Some writers, less inclined to fully research their material, get things wrong.

OTHER PEOPLE

Older books about writing often advise authors who are carrying out research to conduct interviews with recognized experts. If you have a friendly expert to hand, or if you have credentials that open doors, or if you're just the kind of person that doesn't mind putting herself out there, an open conversation can be the most effective non-experiential source available. However, there is a real knack to effective interviewing and it can be a difficult job, even for the professionals.

With all the information that is out there and easily available on the Internet, it's less likely that new writers today will feel the need to interview an expert on sexual issues. We advise having a look at related blogs first, at least early on in your writing career. Many bloggers are happy to interact with readers. The blog may include a link to a specific and related discussion forum. A word of warning, though: there is a distinct difference in tone and in content between an information website and a sex site. For example, it's possible to find advice about polyamory on an information site, and a couple of clicks can take you to a sex site where you will be showered with offers of hot sex, right now. (Polyamory is one alternative to monogamy, and involves close and possibly intimate relationships between three or more people, all having given their consent.)

Of course, you may know someone who isn't publicly recognized as an expert, but who has a wealth of experience in your chosen field. If they're willing to share, opposite-sex partners or good friends can provide the details that add the ring of truth to your fiction. Best friends' adventures, recounted freely over a bottle or two, might be the very material you need. Can you remember exactly what she said, though? Can you ask for more information or clarification when you're both sober? You should definitely get her approval to use her anecdotes, especially if you want to stay friends. And it would be wise to check up on the facts about any sexual act described to you by a confidante.

New experiences

As we keep saying, stay in your comfort zone until the time is right. But when you're up for it, there are all sorts of ways of gaining experience and knowledge. Not just in that way. Although that counts, too.

Let's start with that sexual act that you identified at the end of the sexual memory questions – you remember, the thing that you wished you'd tried? If you have a partner who's open to suggestion, or if it's a solo act that just takes a bit of planning to set up, you could go about making that fantasy happen. As always, research properly and follow safety guidance. Read up on and consider the potential emotional fall out; both successful and unsuccessful attempts to realize fantasies can bring their own complications to a relationship and to your peace of mind.

Set up erotic dates, whether they are on your own or with a significant other:

- **Innovate.** Look for objects that you already have in your home that could be used for erotic purposes, such as wooden spoons or hairbrushes that could be used for spanking. Then use them.

- **Set the scene.** Try introducing new elements to your sex life, whether it's accompanied or solo. Those old favourites of music and candlelight are old favourites for a reason. Create a sexy playlist and a warm glow. Listen to the playlist again when you write.

- **Say it … out loud.** With a partner, either have a go at describing your own fantasies to each other, or read erotic fiction aloud at bedtime.

- **Go shopping.** Ann Summers shops can be found throughout Britain, and sell lingerie, sexy fancy dress and sex toys. If the nearest one is too far from your home, you could book an Ann Summers (or equivalent) party and invite friends round, or order from their website. Again, is there something you've never tried but quite fancy? It's research, after all.

- **See a show.** Burlesque is friendly, often funny, and not too challenging. Sit where you can pay attention to both the performers (beautiful bodies have wobbly bits, too) and the audience (rapt attention one minute, giggling the next).

- **Mix with the like-minded.** Is there a specialist club or pub that you could try out? Or a big event you could attend? Get a ticket and go. National conventions and trade shows, such as the huge annual Erotica events in London, can be a real eye-opener and provide a safe and secure environment. But always be aware of what you are getting yourself into – don't attend events alone if you feel at all nervous.
- **Give it a go.** Also in London, designer lingerie and sex toy shop Coco de Mer runs 'erotic education' events for the sexually adventurous. There may well be something similar near you, or via the Internet.

Of course, there are many, many more things that you can try, and any good general sex manual will have lots of suggestions. Anything written by Tracey Cox will be a good place to start (traceycox.com), or Emily Dubberley. Remember that this is about getting new information as research for your own work. After you've tried something out for the first time, reflect on what you've experienced and make notes about specific sensual and emotional details. It's a double pay-off for your efforts – sexy fun and better erotic fiction.

Lily Harlem, author

'You don't have to hang upside down and be thrashed by a gorgeous vampire and then shagged senseless by him and his best friend to be able to write about it. But if you're going to include BDSM tools of the trade in your story, undertake some online research. There are a lot of people out there who understand and live the lifestyle. You've got to get it right or you'll be snickered at.'

Focus points

We've looked at how to carry out research to find the details that inspire, structure and add credibility to your erotic fiction. As a writer, the best way to generate interest in a subject is to display that interest yourself.

Things to remember

- Don't get lost in research, and don't try to cram every last ounce of your research into the story.
- First times are significant events and often make for good stories.
- There are many emotions at play during erotic encounters.
- You have a lot of emotional experience to draw on, and it's likely that you have plenty of sexual experience, too.
- You don't have to limit yourself to writing what you know.
- If you don't have personal experience to draw upon, don't make too big a leap into the unknown. Do your research.
- Real-life situations may need to be adapted to succeed in fiction.

Things to do

- Make good, clear notes for all of your research, including dates and sources.
- Keep growing your list of emotions and thinking about how each new item could relate to a sexual encounter.
- Taking all due care, look on the Internet for information about sexual acts or orientations that interest you. Non-fiction books are also good sources.
- Make sure that you fully understand safe sexual practices for your subject matter.
- Decide what you are going to do by the end of this week to extend your erotic knowledge.

Where to next?

Throughout this chapter, we've been focusing on sex-related expertise. However, much of what we've covered can apply to your research into other areas, such as hot-air ballooning, or even the skills needed for creative writing.

It's time to move on to Skill Set 2. We'll start to develop your good ideas in Chapter 4 – Storytelling.

4

Storytelling

Story is a fundamental aspect of humanity. We create stories to give meaning to events and to our lives, to explain the unknown and to help us understand what's happening both in and around us. We love story so much that we spend vast resources satisfying our hunger for it. TV, film, books, news, gossip, white lies; it would be terrifying to work out the proportion of an average human lifespan that is used up in creating, shaping, spreading and receiving stories, never mind the sobering thought of how much money we spend on its commercial incarnations.

'Two People Meet'

Here's an old favourite: two people meet and fall in love. Adapted for erotic fiction: two people meet and have sex. Neither of these people is you.

- Who are these people? Do they already know each other? What do they think about each other?
- Where and when do they meet up?
- What do they talk about? What do they avoid talking about?
- What's making things difficult for them?
- Who makes the first move? How?
- What changes things?
- What do they do next?
- What happens in the end? (As well as *that*.)
- What different emotional states does your main character go through?

Plan this story out, adding as much detail to your plan that you can think of without going into full writing. Do you want to write this story? If the answer is no, perhaps you haven't found answers that fully engage your interest. Change your least interesting answers. Don't pick the first thing that comes into your mind. If you're stuck, you could add some items from your Big Sexy List. Do whatever it takes to make this story interesting enough for you to write.

If you're still resisting, is it because you think that you don't have the storytelling skills? We're going to look at storytelling in this chapter, but you already have lots of experience of story.

Are you worried about wordcraft – writing well? That's Chapter 7. And the only way to really improve is to write. Put these fears to the side for a while. No one else has to read what you've written.

Write it. Aim for 1,600 words – 400 beginning, 800 middle, 400 end.

In the exercises at the start of previous chapters, we looked at factual details (things that really do turn you on) and real-life events. We turn now to fiction and the elements that are woven together to make stories work.

Story and causality

Story assumes a connection between events – one thing causes another thing to happen. This is called causality. In a creation story, a god's semen is spilled on the ground and causes life on Earth. In another story, a woman smiles, and this causes a man to lean in and kiss her, which in turn causes her to slap his face. (How often do you slap faces? Have you ever slapped anyone for kissing you? Yet how often do we see this happen in stories?)

We could go back in time – what caused the woman to smile? Or forward – is the man going to get drunk to cope with the rejection, which causes him to crash his car, which causes ... and so on. We could go deeper. Did the kiss cause the slap? Or was it because she suddenly smelled his aftershave, the brand that her abusive ex forced her to drink? Or we could go higher, above the level of the events – the next day the man tells his mates simply that the date didn't work out, skipping the smiling and kissing and slapping altogether. He reframes the story to suit his own purposes. But the whole sorry tale causes him to mistrust the girl-next-door's flirtatious overtures. And so on, and so on.

Writers have to make many decisions about aspects of story – what events, what causality, what happened before or after, whether we're going deeper or higher. The good news is that, because we are so immersed in story from birth, we can do a lot of this without having to think about it. The bad news is that, if we don't think about it, we run the risk of doing it badly, in a clichéd, slapping-across-the-face, first-thing-that-comes-to-mind sort of way. Not good for the story. Not good for the reader. So it's important to think about how story works.

Fiction's trump card

Fiction is a form of entertainment. Erotic fiction is up against all of the other forms of entertainment that are so readily available. What makes you, as a reader, choose erotic fiction over everything else that you could be doing with your time and money?

Compared with the other forms of creativity, such as dance, music, painting and film-making, written fiction has a trump card. It gives its audience direct access to the thoughts of another person. Although this can be accomplished in theatre by techniques such as soliloquies and asides, and in film by voice-overs, these techniques often feel mannered and artificial when bolted on to primarily visual media. In fiction, there's no awkwardness. Characters' thoughts are part of what makes creative writing work.

By allowing access to another mind, fiction provides escape. The reader leaves her own life and its familiar causalities, and takes a break in someone else's head for the duration of the story. We love it when a book takes over. We lose track of real time, living with the characters through the story's events, feeling at least a simulation of their emotions, sharing their fears and joys. Brilliant. This is what we're looking for when we scan the bookshop shelves and tables. We're looking to try on someone else's life for a while. In erotic fiction, at the very minimum, we're looking to try on their sex life.

Readers want to escape into story. They want to pay their money and spend their valuable leisure time following a writer through a world she has invented, in the minds and in the company of people she has created. They just have to find the right story. But there's an overwhelming amount of choice, and readers don't have time to check out all the options. Based on previous reading experiences, they'll look for a writer they can trust.

Trusting the writer

If you are a brand-new writer, the story-hungry reader doesn't know whether she can trust you or not. So she starts to look for clues. You make promises to potential readers by your choice of cover, title and jacket blurb; these must give good indications of the book's subject matter, sub-genre and heat level. So, *Hot Sluts* would be a different reading experience from *The Princess's Private Pleasures*. If the reader likes the signals, she'll try a sample. That's why it's essential to get your first sentence right, and your first paragraph, and your first page. If she still likes what she sees, game on.

That's just the start. To turn reader interest into reader trust, your story must honour the promises you made on the cover and in the sample that she's tested. If it looks like a sizzling cowboy ménage, it had better turn out to be just that. It's fun to stretch sub-genres, but don't you dare mess with the fundamentals.

Creating and maintaining trust are vital, and that's why it's crucial for you to know and respect the conventions of the sub-genre before you put your work in front of a reader. If you're taking the reader's resources – whether that's time, money or both – you have a responsibility to deliver to the best of your abilities.

Trusting the reader

At a superficial level, writers can have few expectations of their readers. The writer supplies the story, and she hopes the reader is entertained. However, the writer must respect her readers' sophistication and intelligence. New writers often haven't learned to trust the reader, yet. They like to explain. They repeat themselves. This may be for the following reasons:

- They don't trust their own writing to have carried the point, so they say it again. For example, if we're told that Tom checks that he has a condom in his wallet before he leaves the house, it really doesn't need to be mentioned again until it's put to use. We'll remember he's equipped.
- They underestimate a reader's ability to pick up small clues. So, if Dick hesitates before kissing the girl, we'll guess that he's nervous and a bit scared of rejection if that's how his character has been set up. We don't need to be told that 'he was really worried that she might think he was disgusting'.
- They don't realize that they're repeating themselves. For example: 'You're such a pig!' she screamed angrily at the top of her voice. If your character says that, we can guess that she's angry. If she's screaming, we don't need to be told it's at the top of her voice. The exclamation mark gives away the loudness, anyway. It might be enough just to leave it at 'You're such a pig!' and move on to poor Harry's response.

The result of all this over-explanation, whether it's deliberate or not, is that the reader feels patronized.

To sum up, the writer makes promises and must deliver on them, while trusting the reader to get the message. The reader gets the message, receives the promised pay-off for her investment of time and possibly money, and learns to trust the writer. Mutual trust leads to a happy partnership, with more sales down the line. That's a great HEA.

The fiction illusion

- From your favourite erotic story, which scene do you remember most vividly?
- What exactly do you remember about it? Perhaps it was a place, a flash of sensory detail, someone doing something to someone else, and that someone else loving it.
- But what did you really see when you read the scene?

All that you 'saw' was a row of marks against background. Letter symbols stand in for sounds. Sounds make up words. Words are symbols in turn, standing in for real-life things. 'A stocking' isn't actually a stocking. It's squiggles of ink on paper, or dark on light if you're e-reading. You translate the words 'a stocking' into an image in your mind. And if stockings turn you on, the image prompted by the word can turn you on, too. So, in the vivid scene from your favourite erotic story, you didn't actually see what you remember 'seeing', and you didn't remember what you actually saw. Prompted by the words used by the writer, you imagined it all. The reader screens the story in her mind.

The things you notice

Take ten seconds to look around you. Do it now.

You probably didn't just smoothly gaze at your surroundings, your sight sweeping from left to right. It is likely that your eyes darted from one detail to the next, noticing the way light falls there, seeing something moving, spotting an item out of place, or an interesting shape, or a different texture.

For three seconds, close your eyes and think of the room. What do you remember most clearly? Why did that particular thing catch your eye?

Now take ten seconds to look at all the green things in the room.

> This time, your eyes probably scanned for objects that fit the category of green. You may have noticed completely different details about the same room.

Just as we've directed you to look for green, the writer directs the reader's inner gaze, allowing it to rest on what's significant. For example, if her characters meet in a crowded bar, and she draws your attention to a shady corner, this corner needs to be where something happens later on. If that corner turns out not to be significant after all, and it's just that she was getting a bit carried away, or didn't understand the implications of what she was doing, the reader experiences a small breach of trust.

Fictional images

- Thinking back to your fictional story from the start of this chapter, what images did you choose to convey to the reader? How did you decide what to include?
- Look back at your writing. Is there anything you've included that should really have been left out? Or anything you could have made more of?
- Now find a memorable scene by a writer you love.
- Read it *as a writer*. Notice what the writer includes and what she leaves out.
- Again, is there anything that should have been left out? Anything that she could have made more of?
- Is there anything that you've learned from this other writer's work that you might want to use in your own writing? Make a note of it.

Your story can't include every possible detail. You'll get bogged down and it will be boring. And don't include random details – make sure they support what you're trying to do creatively. Everything that you include needs to be there for a reason.

Elements of fiction

Story works when words on the page create a flow of images in the reader's mind. But what is story made of? Not everyone agrees on the main elements, but here are the major candidates.

CHARACTER

Stories are about people. Someone's life is changed by events. Over the course of a whole novel, a significant event might change your character's path for ever. In a short story, the change may be subtle, perhaps hinting at further change to come.

The character who changes the most is usually the lead, the focus of the story, the character who makes things happen. Other characters have specific roles, such as the love interest. Despite its romantic connotations, we use 'love interest' to indicate the character on the receiving end of the lead's sexual attention. Another major character is the antagonist, the person who stands against the lead's goals. Sometimes, the antagonist and the love interest are the same person, and sparks fly. Sometimes, there's more than one love interest, or more than one antagonist. There are other character types, such as the best friend or the mentor, each with their own role to play. In creating characters, we ask: 'Who is the story about?'

PLOT

Plot is what happens to your characters. Events in themselves don't necessarily matter – they just 'are'. What matters is how we react to those events. Different people react to the same things in different ways – while one character will accept a sexual invitation, another will run for the hills. Therefore, a strong plot is tied to the particular character that you are writing about – plot and lead character are different sides of the same coin. The events in your plot are tailored to challenge your lead. Your lead is developed as someone who will respond to the story's events in a way that will entertain the reader. Plot answers the question: 'What happens to the characters?'

SETTING

Erotic fiction often pays particular attention to setting. In the most general terms, it's where the story takes place – exotic settings such as private islands, tolerant settings such as BDSM dungeons, transgressive settings such as the local police station. The story will be affected by its era – *when* it takes place. If two stories take place in New York, a story set in the pre-AIDS era of the mid-1970s will differ significantly from a story set a decade later.

Setting also refers to the social, political and moral issues of the story world. Because erotic fiction often deals with transgression, these factors come into their own. If your story takes place in a society that proscribes particular sexual activities, yet your character just can't help herself, her transgressions add conflict and therefore a frisson to the action. In choosing a setting, we ask 'Where?', 'When?' and 'What is life like?'

Theme

Some writers know the deeper meaning in their fiction before they start writing. A story about 'two people meeting and having sex' may actually be about the alienation affecting urban singletons, or the limitations on women's expectations despite social and political changes, or the search for life's meaning. Many writers revisit the same themes repeatedly in their work. A new writer may not be aware of her theme until she can look back on a body of fiction.

If you know which deeper theme you want to write about, be careful. If it's an issue you feel strongly about, you're in danger of emphasizing theme to the detriment of story. Avoid propaganda.

If you don't know what your theme is, don't worry. It might emerge when the first full draft is complete. At any stage, you can change your story to ensure that your theme is supported by your character and plot choices. The key question for theme is 'What's the story *really* about?'

POINT OF VIEW

Who is telling the story? That's the point of view (POV).

Usually, the lead is the POV character. The reader directly experiences only those things that the POV character senses, thinks and feels. She can't get into anyone else's thoughts in that scene. Just as you were primed to notice green things when you applied a green filter, your POV character will be primed to notice things that are important to her. Sometimes, other characters will take over the POV for scenes, letting us find out about the other side of the story and get into someone else's thoughts.

Narrative voice is about the POV's position in relation to the story. There are many options, but the following two are popular in erotic fiction.

- **First person.** This is when the story is about 'me'. For example, 'He trailed his tongue along the sole of my foot. I shivered.' The upside of this is that some writers find it easier to think about what happens and how the character might react if they are putting themselves in the character's place. The downside is that the writer can become too close to the character, getting bogged down in her thoughts and reactions.

- **Close third person.** This is when the story is about 'her' as the main POV character. In these, you would see: 'He trailed his tongue along the sole of her foot. She shivered.' The 'close' part refers to the fact that we can get into the POV character's thoughts, just as we can in first person, but we can't get into anyone else's for that scene. We can jump into someone else's head when the scene changes. Close third person is the most common storytelling voice.

Other narrative voice options, such as omniscient (getting into everyone's head and knowing everything that happens) and second person (things happen to 'you'), are not common choices in the modern market.

Some writers change narrative voice and POV character within a story. For example, the lead's story may be told in first person, and the subplots relating to other characters in third person. Whatever you choose, the rule is to be consistent.

The key point to remember is that the POV character provides the filter. So, if your POV character in a particular scene is an 18-year-old virgin, she will react to the environment and the antagonist's sexual overtures in a different way from the experienced professional dominatrix in the next scene.

 Victoria Blisse, author

'Don't forget that an erotic story is not all just sex, sex, sex, sex, sex. You need to have two other very important elements. First, characters your readers will love. Make sure to flesh them out so your readers will care what happens to them. Second, a good plot. You need something that drives the action, is believable and exciting and that can have a sexual element to it but shouldn't just be about getting your characters laid.'

Scenes

We've mentioned scenes a few times now. The scene is the basic building block of storytelling. In scenes, we show characters in a setting, being affected by plot. Writers on writing all have their own views about the finer points of how to define scenes, but the existence of scenes and the need for them is not in question. One of our strongest recommendations for beginning writers is that they learn how to think and write in scenes.

SCENE BEGINNING

In the beginning of the scene, we find out where and when the scene takes place, which character has the point of view, and what that character's intentions are (her goal). We set up the rest of the scene, making sure that the reader has enough information to understand what happens later and its implications. The length of the beginning is entirely dependent on how much information you need to convey. It helps to think about what the character has been doing immediately before the scene starts, as that will influence factors such as how the character is feeling, what she is thinking about, and how she is dressed.

The beginning of a scene is not the place to go into lengthy explanations about the character's background or descriptions about the setting. In erotic fiction, we don't need justification for the character's behaviour. We will assume she is a positive sexual being who enjoys whatever she does.

Assess the scene beginning

Look at your story from the start of this chapter. Did you include enough information at the start to let your reader know who, where and when? Did you state what your character's intentions were? If not, make notes now about how you can include this information.

SCENE MIDDLE

In the middle of the scene, the character's intentions are challenged. Things don't go to plan. If she's looking for a kiss, she ends up in a fight. If she's desperate for an early night, Mr Right appears and he's leaving at dawn. This is conflict. A story without conflict is deadly boring, and often represents wish-fulfilment for the writer, with no insight into what keeps the reader engaged. How much conflict is there in porn? None – nothing gets in the way of the sex. But the best stories, like the best gossip, are about things going wrong.

The scene middle is where the action of the story plays out. Your character's intentions are scuppered, so what does she do? Does she go along with it? Or does she try to get back on track? Your character's decisions reveal her personality to the reader and to the other people in the story.

The actions that your character takes in response to the conflict are links in the chain of cause and effect. Mr Right turning up causes her to stay in the bar, chatting and flirting, which causes her to miss the last train home. The scene's action might be physical (flirty touching), or it might be dialogue (chatting), or it might be thinking about her situation and trying to decide what to do. The action of the scene moves the story on. Something changes for the POV character.

Assess the scene middle

What's the conflict in your story? Don't worry if you think conflict is missing – you can rewrite it in. Take the action that occurs in the middle of your scene. How could this have been the result of conflict, something your character didn't actually want to happen at that time? Sometimes it's easiest to keep the middle (because that's the meat of the scene, the juicy stuff you really want to write about) and to rewrite the beginning, setting the scene up with different character intentions. So, if the middle of your scene is about your lead being spanked by her driving instructor, don't let her get into that car with submission on her mind. Begin the scene with her being relieved that the new driving instructor is a cute young woman, because she has sworn off alpha males.

SCENE END

Scenes should end with the character in a different situation from the one she was in at the start. She might have obtained something, such as a physical object or a piece of knowledge, or she might have lost something or someone. She will have either have failed to achieve what she set out to do, and she'll be trying to find a different way to do it, or she'll have succeeded but the success throws up another complication. Scenes end with the reader wondering what happens next. That's the reason they'll keep reading.

Assess the scene end

Look at the end of your scenes. What question do you leave the reader with? Is it who, what, why, when, where or how?

The flow of time

Scenes don't have a set length. They can be as short or as long as you need them to be. It all depends on how much detail you need to include so that the reader understands what's happening, is engaged by the action, appreciates that something has changed, and is left wondering what happens next.

But a crucial aspect of writing in scenes is that we are representing the natural flow of time. As the scene starts, the clock starts ticking.

In a scene:

- **Don't jump around in different time periods** – it's much harder to read. Write about what is happening now for your character, as it happens, in order. If you have to mention things that happened in the past, present these in chronological order.

- **Avoid flashbacks.** The past is not as gripping as what's going on for your character right now. (Unless a strand of your story takes place in the past. In this case, that past time is the present for the characters in that part of the story, and full scenes will be set in that 'when'.)

- **Don't let the character pause to think at length, especially during conversations.** If one character says 'How are you?' and the other character thinks about how she ended up with the sore head that she had when she got up that morning, and what happened on the overcrowded train carriage on her way to work, and the bunch of daffodils that her colleague left on her desk, and isn't he cute? – all before she gets round to saying 'Fine, thanks' – the flow of time has been disrupted. This might flash through her mind in an instant, but it takes a long time to read, and remember we're tracking real time, with the ticking clock. We generally don't take lengthy pauses before answering questions in conversations. Of course, your character might talk about all of these things, but would that amount of detail be interesting and move your story forward?

- **Don't let the boring stuff play out second by second.** You can gloss over things the reader already knows or doesn't need to know. If nothing of interest happens on the morning commute, you can skip it by saying 'Half an hour later, Penny stepped down from the train.' Then something significant can happen at the station to move the scene and the story forward.

Assess the flow of time

How have you handled time in the first scene of your story? Does it flow forward, or do you jump about? Have you given the right amount of page time to events? For example, writing second-by-second, you can't fit a full three-course meal into a 2,000-word scene. But by summarizing the boring bits, you can cover in detail the life-changing thing that happened under the table between the main course and dessert.

Making a scene

- Pick a sexual activity that you'd be interested in reading about, an activity that involves two participants.
- Create your characters. Build in some points of opposition – for example, one is rich, the other penniless. Old, young. Innocent, experienced. What are their ages, genders, backgrounds?
- Decide your characters' intentions for the start of the scene. Make them want different things, introducing conflict.
- Decide who is going to be your POV character. How would that character's filter be different from your own?
- Choose a setting that will add an element of external conflict, such as a dangerous setting, or one with no privacy, or one that triggers a specific non-sexual reaction in at least one of your characters.
- Identify the five or six main events or steps of the scene, the things that happen in chronological order. The first event should be before the sexual action takes place, but they need to be erotically involved by step 3 at the latest.
- Decide what question you want your reader to come away with, in relation to who, what, why, when, where or how.
- If you know what your own enduring theme is, then look at the choices you've made so far in this exercise and understand how they might fit in to an exploration of that theme. If you don't know your own bigger question yet, it's not likely to become apparent in planning one

isolated scene. But if you'd like to think about theme in relation to your writing, you might want to borrow one of the three themes that we mentioned earlier: alienation in the city, the limits on women's expectations, or the meaning of life. What would you have to change in your scene to reflect your chosen theme?

• What would the scene after this one be?

 ## Victoria Blisse, author

'Write what you want to write. It's tempting to try and write what seems to be selling well at the time but that is going to be fruitless in the end. You've got to let the story out that's inside you. Those are the best ones.'

Focus points

You've been surrounded by stories all your life. If you understand what stories are made of, it's easier to make sure that your own stories work.

Things to remember

- In story, events are related by causality.
- The writer decides what goes into the story and the order in which things are revealed.
- The reader screens the story in her mind, based on details revealed by the writer.
- The elements of fiction include character, plot, setting, theme and point of view.
- Stories are told in scenes.
- In scenes, time flows naturally in one direction.

Things to do

- Again, know the conventions of your sub-genre so that you can earn and retain your readers' trust.
- Build your understanding of point of view by applying different character filters in your day-to-day life. For example, see the supermarket trip or the commute to work through one of your character's eyes. What would she do differently?
- In your reading, pay attention to what the writer includes in detail, and what she skips over.
- When you get to the end of a scene that you are reading or watching, notice what question keeps you in the story. Does it relate to who, what, why, when, where or how?

Where to next?

In this chapter we've touched on subjects that have many books written about them. We wanted to raise these topics in your consciousness so that you can begin to make informed decisions about what events and facts to include, and when.

In Chapter 5 we are going to look in more detail at one of the most important aspects of writing fiction – creating characters.

5

Characters

It's not unknown for us to get towards the end of an erotic novel and to find that we're skimming or skipping the sex scenes because, frankly, they're not always that well written and we've seen it all before. So, when the sex palls, what keeps us reading?

What we really want to know is how it all ends up for the characters; will they sort things out by the end? Will they be OK? Strange as it may seem, we've fallen a little bit in love with people who are nothing more than a series of marks on a page, marks that prompt images in our minds, images that are linked together into scenes that build to make a story about people we've come to care about. Sometimes, we've fallen a big bit in love.

In Chapter 8 we'll think about ways to 'skip-proof' your sex scenes. But this chapter is about creating characters that your reader will love. And characters that they'll hate, or feel sorry for, or even forget completely once they turn the page, because there are different kinds of character in fiction, with different functions to fulfil.

Characters you have loved

- Do you have any characters from written fiction on your Big Sexy List? Did you fall a little bit in love with any of them? Or with any other character in your reading history?
- What did you like about those characters? Think about their personality and how they reacted to other characters and to story events. What, if anything, did you dislike?
- What made you fall in love? This is such an important question. It's worth hooking up with a loved character again, by going back to the book where you originally met. Find out how the writer managed to manipulate you into adoring their creation. Reread it, now that you're a writer yourself. Don't get sucked into the story again if you can help it.

What story needs from your characters

Regardless of genre, story requires certain things from your characters:

- **Characters must be capable of doing what's required of them by the plot.** A three-day trek across the Scottish Highlands in the dead of winter will make specific physical demands. A striptease in front of the local rugby or soccer team requires certain psychological characteristics. The reader needs to believe that your character can and would do what you're making her do. While it can be fun to write against type – accountant by day, stripper by night – the capability still needs to be there.
- **Characters need to be consistent.** 'Factual' details, such as eye colour, mustn't change through the story. Keeping track of characteristics, ages and experiences might not be difficult in a short story, but it can be challenging for novelists, and it is no small feat for serial writers. This is true for psychological factors, too. A character presented as a nice guy and a valid love interest won't kick the leading lady's dog or have sex with her sister (unless everyone's informed, consenting and turned on by the idea, of course).

- **Characters need to be affected by what's happening in the story.** We're interested in how events impact upon other people. How do they react? Is that the right way to react? How would we have reacted in the same circumstances? At the end of the story, events will have changed the major characters in some way. But this has to be done incrementally and logically, so that character consistency isn't stretched beyond breaking point.

If you create characters who are capable, consistent and who react realistically to events, they will be believable.

Victoria Blisse, author

'Writing believable characters can be hard, but knowing your character well can help. Don't just think about hair and eye colour, build and height. What kind of music does he or she like? Do they have hobbies or personality quirks that you can bring out in the story? What does your leading lady hate? What is her favourite colour? What football team does your hero support? Where was he born? Does he have brothers and sisters? You may not need to write these facts into the story, but knowing your character well will make your portrayal of them more believable.'

Kinds of character

You take the lead role in your own life, with all the people that surround you – family, friends, colleagues, the cute barman in your local pub or bar – affecting your life with different degrees of impact. Similarly, you will generally find one character who takes on the lead role in a story. Around the lead will be a couple of other primary characters who have a major impact on her life, a handful of secondary characters who have some impact, and as many minor characters as are needed to populate the story world.

THE LEAD CHARACTER

The lead character is the story's focal point. She is facing a problem; perhaps she's consigned to the life of a servant, forced to clean up after her stepmother and sisters, and she's starved of love. Something happens in her world, and she reacts; the invitation to the ball arrives, and she wants to go. Her actions determine the course of the story; she proves herself worthy and earns a pumpkin carriage, glass slippers and the prince's embrace. She encounters problems along the way – a lost slipper, her true identity a mystery. By the end, she has succeeded and she has been changed by events; she gets her prince and her HEA. Problem solved.

The lead character is the writer's way into her topic. You might know that you want to write about swinging clubs. As soon as you conceive of a lead character, the story begins to coalesce as she becomes the focal point for everything you've learned through research. Your character starts from a position of ignorance and goes on a journey of discovery, just as you did. And she'll end up a different person, knowing more, seeing things through new eyes. So this gives you ideas for the beginning, middle and ending of your story.

The lead is also the reader's way in to the story, and there are different ways of handling this. Some books set the lead up as an 'everywoman', an average female (if slightly better looking) on to whom the reader can project her own personality, fantasizing herself into the story. She wants to be wooed by Prince Charming, or to have a go at swinging. This places all the weight of interest on the other characters and the plot. Other books have larger-than-life, individual and distinct lead characters. In these, it's harder for the reader to wish herself directly into the story, but she'll be reading to find out how the fascinating lead copes with it all, and she'll be expecting reactions to story events that are plausible even if they are skewed away from how the reader might react herself.

Whether she's an everywoman or an individual, she has to be likeable enough for the reader to want to spend time with her. This doesn't mean that she should be flawless, but there have to be enough positives in her character to outweigh the negatives. A virtue such as courage, curiosity or self-awareness will make up for bad attitudes and habits. You will want the reader to be on the lead's side from the very first page, so make sure that you pick a strong virtue for your character and show it from the outset.

The lead character gets the most time on the page. She may be the only POV character in the book. She'll be the most complex character, perhaps with conflicting desires and divided loyalties, and with character traits that depend upon who she's with and what she's doing. The lead will be drawn in fine detail.

THE ANTAGONIST

If there is one, the baddie in the story is regarded as the second most important of the primary characters in most genres. This character is known as the villain or the antagonist. She may be the cause of the lead character's problems and will certainly oppose her goals (the wicked stepmother). In modern adult stories, the antagonist isn't just plain bad, and doesn't oppose the lead character just to mess things up. She'll do what she thinks is right from her position as the lead in her own story. In fact, your lead character is the antagonist's antagonist. Therefore, it's worth spending as much time and care developing the antagonist as in creating the lead.

Sometimes, the antagonist role, standing against the lead's goals, is taken by different characters at different times in the story.

THE LOVE INTEREST

The next important primary character in most fiction is the love interest, if there is one (the handsome prince). Many stories conflate the roles of the antagonist and the love interest, creating a character that the lead initially clashes with, but eventually comes to love. Often, the love interest won't be looking for the same thing as the lead character. They both fall in love in spite of what they think they want. Erotic fiction is different from other fiction in that the love interest is always a more important character than the antagonist (except when the same character fulfils both roles).

The love interest and the antagonist get less page time than the lead, but more than everyone else. They may have their own subplots, played out in scenes where they hold the point of view. The lead character might not appear in those scenes. Long scenes may be split in half, with the lead taking us so far, then the love interest taking over. Remember that we only get direct access to the POV character's emotions. Swapping POV halfway through a significant scene lets us know what the other partner is thinking. Indicate a POV change to the reader by using a double line space.

Finally, there may be more than one love interest, depending on the sub-genre.

SECONDARY CHARACTERS

Beyond the big three of the lead, the antagonist and the love interest, other characters influence the plot. Some of them will help the lead character, such as sidekicks and mentors (the fairy godmother). Some will hinder her, such as friends who unwittingly give bad advice, or the antagonist's henchmen (the ugly sisters).

Secondary characters have their own motivation for being involved in the lead character's struggles – remember that they are the lead in their own lives. They are not as complicated as the primary characters. They often have straightforward motivations and are characterized more simply, with no deep contradictions. They appear in the primary characters' scenes rather than having scenes of their own. This stops them from becoming too important in the story.

MINOR CHARACTERS

Minor characters are needed to make the story work. They are functionaries such as the waitress who takes the order or the soldiers who die on the battlefield (the mice who turn into footmen). They are nameless and described in very broad strokes, if at all. Don't put too much detail into your minor characters. If you make them too individual, the reader will assume they're important and pay attention, expecting them to crop up again later in the story. Don't let minor characters have their own way, no matter how interesting you find them, or how well you've written the scene.

NARRATOR

Sometime a writer will employ a narrator who is a character in their own right. This is helpful if the lead character is unusual and the average person's take on their exploits is needed. Famous examples are Watson's reporting of Holmes's methods, and Nick Carraway's narration of events in *The Great Gatsby*. Difficulties arise because the narrator must either be present for every scene with the lead, which is impractical, or they must find out about the lead's actions second-hand, which is not dramatic. Erotic fiction doesn't normally employ narrators; we want the immediacy of the lead's emotions, not have them filtered through someone else.

M.K. Elliot, author

'We all like our erotic fiction to leave us squirming in our seats or even taking part in a little one-handed reading, but the sex in erotic fiction is so much more than that. When done well, it's about growing the characters – their relationship with each other and within themselves. It's about building trust and discovering a side of themselves that they may not have known about before.'

What erotic fiction needs from your characters

The most important thing about the lead character and the love interest in your own erotic fiction is that you find them attractive. This will come across in your writing.

If you are writing for yourself or you don't expect to sell your work, you can do what you like regarding characters. However, if you are writing for the market, you need to know its conventions and preferences.

ESSENTIAL FEATURES

The primary characters in commercial erotic fiction – male and female – need four essential features:

1 Beauty

We don't all define beauty in the same way. But, as a society, we love beautiful people. It's some combination of biology and aesthetics.

If the POV character thinks their partner is beautiful, we'll go along with it. And if we get some descriptive details and it happens to turn out that we think that's beautiful, too, so much the better.

But we're not restricted to conventional beauty. Unconventional is good, particularly for unconventional characters. And some erotic fiction celebrates specific body types, notably the Rubenesque in stories about curvy ladies.

2 Strength

Male characters certainly have physical strength, and the females often display some in times of need. They need their strength and stamina for all the sex. And there's bravery, too. They tend to cope with pain and discomfort well, and often enjoy it.

Strength of character is essential. While emotions may run strong, these characters cannot be overly emotional or sensitive.

If you're hoping for the biggest possible audience, readers tend to prefer men who are not submissive, and women who are not dominant. However, there are many successful stories that show the opposite.

3 Vulnerability

However strong your characters, when they meet the right partner, they let their vulnerable side show. Characters might not notice this vulnerability creeping in, but the readers will. Characters might deny it, or fight against it. No good ever comes of that in genre fiction. They find themselves becoming more tangled than ever.

Vulnerability provokes more strength, with the character protecting their partner and fending off any threat to the emotional or sexual relationship.

Characters are often written with emotional vulnerability originating from events in their past, the backstory. This can work well, as long as you don't muddle symptoms of vulnerability with sexual preferences. For example, sadness and vulnerability may be traced back to the death of a parent in childhood, but this shouldn't be used to 'explain' unconventional sexual practices.

4 Passion

Characters in erotic fiction are sexually open to new partners and new experiences. They are curious. They are often sexually driven, too; they know what they want and they go about getting it.

If they must, they will fight for their relationship, perhaps to the detriment of other parts of their lives. Passionate characters often have strong non-sexual drives, too. They strive to succeed, to protect, to perform. The passion may be well hidden at first but, like vulnerability, it will leak out despite the character's best efforts.

POPULAR MALE CHARACTER TYPES

There are types of primary character males in popular erotic fiction. They might not be to your sexual or creative taste, so think about whether you're going to match these types or step away from them in your own writing. The top three are:

1 The alpha male. Successful, wealthy and used to being in charge, the alpha male is the staple of erotic and romantic fiction, from Mr Darcy to Christian Grey and many, many more in between. Often arrogant, he's ready to be taken down a peg or two.

2 The guy-next-door. This man has hidden depths and they may run undiscovered until late one night you hear a noise in the hallway and you come out on to the landing only to find him carrying an injured kitten into his flat. Despite his worry, he gives you that lop-sided smile and ... well, you get the idea. He's a good guy with quiet, inner strength and lots of caring. He might be a colleague or a friend.

3 The renegade. He doesn't give a damn. He's his own man and won't play by anyone else's rules, and he succeeds on his own terms, not by society's dictate. Whatever he does, he's the best. He often spells danger. Until, uh-oh, an emotional connection shakes him up.

POPULAR FEMALE CHARACTER TYPES

We've found that there's a lot more variety in female character types, but here are three popular ladies for a start. Again, you get to decide whether or not you are going base your characters on these types for greater commercial appeal.

1 Feisty but loveable. These women can certainly take care of themselves, and they'll fight for anything that they love. The combination of strength and a loveable nature is attractive to characters and readers alike.

2 The inexperienced maiden. She might have had sex before, but she never knew how much she was missing. Thank goodness an alpha male is on hand to show her how it's done. She's willing to learn.

3 The sex bomb. An adventuress, this lady knows exactly what she's after and that's variety. She pursues it at every opportunity, striding through her sexual encounters and teaching us a thing or two along the way.

RELATIONSHIPS

The relationship between the lead and the love interest is usually the main source of emotion in your story. Relationships are messy. They are about accommodating each other's foibles and values, and compromising, and finding a way despite it all. It stands to reason that the relationship between the lead and the love interest shouldn't be plain sailing. Apart from that, fiction is driven by conflict. No conflict, no story.

Aside from the individual characteristics of your lead and your love interest, how would you characterize their relationship? There should be conflict, but enough of a spark or burn that they're both willing to overcome any problems.

CHARACTERISTICS TO AVOID

Some characteristics don't get readers on a character's side. The following should be avoided: cruelty, dishonesty (unless she's doing it for a greater good, and then she should be torn about it) and crassness.

And there are a few common characters that we have trouble with. First up is the improbable virgin. She's how old? And she's never ...? But yet she does *that* without blinking an eye? Make sure there's a good reason for virginity, such as she's only just come of age, or there's social or religious pressure that makes sense within the story.

Second, we have the mixed-up genders. If you're writing a gay story, don't write one of the men as though he's a girl with a cock. They both need to be manly. The same applies to lesbian stories. Don't make one a cockless bloke. They're both women.

Finally, Miss or Mr Perfect. Too good to be true. Boring.

DIVERSITY

With the Internet's ability to link people with specific interests all around the world, it's easier than ever to access and circulate erotic fiction that has more of a niche appeal. Greater character diversity is possible. For example, there's a growing interest in erotic fiction about characters with disabilities, or about significantly older characters.

Character creation

Events have meaning only in so far as they affect us. A civil war is a serious and life-changing experience for anyone caught up in it, but it may barely register in the consciousness of the rest of the world as it settles down in front of the evening news.

Character and plot are two sides of the same coin. In creating plot, we devise events that will impact upon the people in our stories. In creating characters, we equip them to find meaning in and be changed by the events of the plot. Storytelling requires that we fit the character to the plot and vice versa – in changing one, we have to change the other. While the Cinderella story has a clear plot, if we remove the passive Cinders and plonk Scarlett O'Hara into the story in her place, we know that the plot will have to change to keep up with her antics. Even if we keep the structure the same – fairy godmother, ball and glass slipper – Scarlett will follow a different path from one to the other.

Some writers prefer to start with plot, and some prefer to start with character. Neither method is better than the other. So that we can set things out clearly, we've separated character and plot into two chapters, but you will find yourself flipping the character/plot coin from one side to the other, as you develop your stories.

A lead not like you

There's no doubt that you will put pieces of yourself into all of the characters that you ever create. Although it may seem the easiest option, it's hard to do justice to a character, and hence your plot, if that character is just a thinly disguised version of yourself. Erotic fiction isn't memoir. The following exercise will help you step away from the known.

1 Describe yourself in six key words or phrases – the things that most define you. An example might be:

- Woman
- 50 years old
- Teacher
- Wife
- Writer
- Caring

These are things that you know how to be.

2 Now find the opposite of each of these descriptions. Don't worry if there isn't a direct opposite – identify something that's very different:

- Man
- 25 years old
- Student
- Single
- Salesman
- Cold-hearted

You will know what it's like to be some of the things on your second list. Anyone who's 50 can remember what it's like to be 25. You might hesitate to admit to some, but even a caring person has been cold-hearted, even if only in defence of those they love.

3 In the last step, you have created a character that's as different as possible from yourself, in relation to the key characteristics that define you. Could you use this as a lead character? If not, change back the one attribute that you would find most difficult to write. For example, it's likely you'd rather write about a character that's the same sex as you, and that's probably a good idea for a beginner. How does this character look now?

4 Now write down another four key words or phrases to describe your own values or beliefs, and their opposites:

- Vegetarian
- Rationalist
- Feminist
- Atheist
- Omnivore
- Dreamer
- Un-politicized
- Believer

We've tweaked these opposites, and you should do the same until you find descriptions that you'd be happy to write about. For example, as an atheist, you might find it impossible to write about a lead that had conventionally religious leanings, but someone who believed in ghosts would be acceptable (and may inspire some interesting erotic plot events).

5 Look at your list of ten descriptors. Give this character a name. Don't sweat over it for now – the first thing that comes to mind is fine as a way of identifying them for now.

This sketch – ten pieces of character description and a name – is a good starting point for building your lead.

WHAT'S YOUR LOVE INTEREST TYPE?

If you've ever heard someone newly in love enthusiastically describe their beloved, then met the object of their affections and wondered what all the fuss was about, you'll know that it's easiest to make someone sound attractive if you find them attractive yourself. When you're creating a love interest, make sure that it's someone that you'd like to fall into bed with.

Think about your type – the kind of partner that you always seem to go for. You might end up getting your heart broken, but there's something about them that you can't resist.

Just as you did in the exercise above, make a list of up to ten descriptors that would sum them up.

If there's anything on your list that would be inappropriate in erotic fiction, either modify it or replace it. So, a male character who is violent towards women won't work in the genre. A gambler might be suitable if he displays risky sexual behaviour that entices your lead, but won't be if he's in a downward spiral that leaves him destitute. Remember that we're looking for upbeat sexual relationships.

Now write as much detail down about your perfect lover as you can. You might want to write it out in prose, or in the format of an interview, but bullet points are fine, too. Are there any points from your Big Sexy List that might be useful here?

Look back over the character you've created. Tweak any of the points you've listed until the mere thought of this character makes you weak at the knees.

FLAWED CHARACTERS

Readers want to see a character react and change during a story. So neither your lead nor your love interest should be perfect, rounded people at the start. Each of them should have at least one flaw, a problem that they need to learn to overcome incrementally through the experience they gain during the course of the story.

If your story shows that it's important for people to be open to new experiences, your lead might start out unwilling to take romantic or sexual risks. If you're writing about commitment, your love interest will be flighty. If you want to write about wild orgies, it's unrealistic to start a short story with a blushing virgin lead (remember the character has to be capable), but your love interest may be the jealous type.

 Lily Harlem, author

'I really believe in making characters who are not perfect. This can be either physically or emotionally or, if that's your storyline, morally. Everyone in real life has baggage, and sometimes bad choices are made, regretted and then redeemed. Because you want your characters to be as realistic as possible, use imperfection to make them stand out in your book. I'm not saying your hero can't be tall, dark and handsome. He can, but give him something extra. For example, I think vulnerability can make a man incredibly sexy. As a writer you can exploit this with dialogue and inner monologue in the build-up to or during a sex scene. This might be showing him emotionally laid bare for her. For example, the hero could have something distressing in his history that means he always likes to be in control. Perhaps she can blindfold him during sex or cuff him to the bed and urge him to give himself over to her completely. The scene then has so much more meaning than if it's just a quick bit of fun bondage, and will be very erotic if you get it right because it's layered. The reader, if they know your character's history, will feel like they are in the head of your hero/heroine and living the moment with them. It's the basis for three-dimensional characters, giving them quirks, fears, strengths, a past and hopes for the future … and three-dimensional is what you're after.'

THE ANTAGONIST AGAIN

You might not have a separate antagonist in your erotic fiction, as the person standing in opposition to the lead is often the love interest. If you do have a separate character, it'll either be someone who strives to keep your lovers apart (a love rival, a parent), or someone who presents a challenge in the world outside their sexual relationship (a business rival, an assassin). Or they do both.

Once you know the role that the antagonist plays in your story, they can be worked up in the same way as the lead and the love interest. Pick their traits to make them capable of fulfilling their role, and make sure there are points of contrast and conflict with the lead and the love interest.

Backstory

How did your characters end up the way they did? To explore their backstory, the things that happened to them before the current story started, use your own backstory as a map.

1 Split your life into seven-year chunks. Write a short paragraph or bullet points to describe what your life was like in the following sections, up to the section that includes your current age. This may take up to an hour. *Warning* – if there are events in your past that have caused you psychological problems, or that may cause you distress, you may wish to skate past those years, or avoid this exercise altogether.

- Birth to six years
- Seven to 13 years
- 14 to 20 years
- 21 to 27 years
- 28 to 34 years
- 35 to 41 years
- 42 to 48 years
- 49 to 55 years
- 56 to 62 years
- 63 to 69 years
- More if you need it

For each section, identify the following:

- The names of major influences – people, ideas, movements

- Life-changing events
- What you loved
- What you hoped for
- What you worried about
- What frightened you
- What you regretted then
- What you regret now.

2 If you haven't done an exercise like this before, it can throw up huge surprises, especially as you summarize your distant past. You might see yourself in a new light. Is there anything missing from this, your life story? Go back and put it in.

3 Now think about the primary characters that you've created – the lead, love interest and antagonist. What happened in the relevant sections of their pasts to bring them to their current place in life? How did they end up with those particular flaws?

4 How will the events of your story affect their current life section?

5 Think forward to the end of the current or next section of your life. What would you like to say about this section when you look back?

Character names

There are websites that will generate character names for you. We don't think that's such a good idea for characters you've created, because names have connotations. To illustrate this, how old are the following characters, and where do they live?

- Eva
- Marguerite
- Doreen
- Tiffany

It's impossible to hear a name without making assumptions about the person's age and social status. So you'll probably want to pick just the right name for your characters. Baby name books help for first names, and writers often look for a name that has a meaning or connotation that is relevant to their character or story. For example, Eden can be used for either male or female characters. It is originally a Hebrew name, and it means 'delight'. Phone books are good for surnames. Check the Internet for real-life holders of names, and consider renaming your characters if need be. Be especially careful with names that are not from your native culture – you may be unaware of connotations.

Be sure to pick names that are easily distinguishable from each other – don't have a Ruby and a Rudy in the same book. Each character's initial can be a different letter.

Character information sheets

Lily Harlem, author

'Erotic romance is simply a romance with the bedroom door left open. There's no "He held her hand and led her up the stairs. The End." The reader gets to find out what the hero is like in bed – if he's good, if he's a praise-the-Lord-in-an-unholy-way kind of guy when he comes or if he's a bite-his-lip-and-groan bloke – yes, every detail is out there, and if you've made your reader fall in love with the hero, then the reader will adore you for these details.'

If you are writing longer fiction or a series, you need to keep track of the facts about your characters, and character information sheets help you organize your details. For shorter fiction or for secondary characters, you might want to use the headings as prompts in character creation.

Use the characteristics or details you identified in the exercises in this chapter as the baseline, and extrapolate from there. Go into as much detail as you like. Add more headings if you find them useful.

- **Identification**
  - Name
  - Date of birth
  - Current age

- **Looks**
  - Hair
  - Eyes
  - Face
  - Skin
  - Body type and shape
  - Distinguishing features and marks
- **How they spend their time**
  - Occupation
  - Seniority
  - Salary
  - Leisure activities
  - Friends
- **How they spend their money**
  - Home
  - Car/transport
  - Clothes
- **The kind of person they are**
  - Major flaw
  - Significant virtue
  - Other characteristics from 'A lead not like you'
- **What made them who they are**
  - Education
  - Upbringing and family
  - Sexual history
  - Cherished belongings

In Chapter 7 – Plot – we will discuss motivation and goals, and you may wish to include these on information sheets, too.

Character tips

We've taken you step by step from a character you know well – yourself – to the creation of brand-new characters. Here are some more suggestions about characters:

- **Don't have too many named, secondary characters in your story** because it becomes hard for readers to follow. You can avoid naming people by referring to them in relation to more important characters, for example 'Kiki's boss' or 'Kiki's mother'. Or you could combine smaller characters' roles, giving more than one story job to each person. So, Kiki's brother who introduces her to the love interest might also be the person who mentions a new burlesque club opening in town.
- **Find short cuts to working out your characters.** Try using the tarot major arcana and face cards for character basics. Or model your lead after your favourite film star. Research archetypes in literature and base your characters on established and recurring story roles such as the mentor, the threshold guardian and the trickster. Or try deciding what animal would represent your character. Without telling the reader, think of this animal when you are describing what the character is doing, or what she looks like. If your character is like a raven, she might have dark, gleaming eyes and a proud but slightly sinister air. How would this come across in the way she moves, or thinks?
- **Don't base characters wholly on yourself or on people you know.** It restricts you unnecessarily as a writer, and there is potential to harm or offend those around you, especially in this genre. Unless, of course, your partner is keen and willing, in which case it might be a bit of a thrill.
- **Don't feel that you have to create swathes of background material** for your character before you start, describing what's in their fridge, or thinking up their first pet's name. You need only those details that are significant within the span and action of your story. You may not know what you're going to need until you're in the middle of writing, so you can create the details when they're required. Add them to your character information sheet to keep track. You need to know your characters without growing tired of them.
- **On the other hand, if any technique helps, go for it.** Backstory like mad if you love it. People-watch if you want to. Just make sure these activities don't keep you away from writing the actual story. You'll find out over time what helps and what hinders.
- **Falling in love with your own characters is a mixed blessing.** On the one hand, it makes the hours you spend writing all the

sweeter. On the other hand, it makes challenging your character through conflict more difficult – you may be tempted to give them an easy ride. If your character doesn't suffer, your story will.

 # Focus points

Creating and getting to know your characters is like any other type of planning for writing. Good planning can save time. It means that you don't have to cast around for what to do or say next and it definitely cuts down the number of drafts needed to get to a final version of a story. So it's worth doing as much as you need to get the story going and to keep it afloat.

However, crafting character histories and complete worlds is not worth doing for its own sake. Why go to lots of trouble for something that'll never end up on the page? Unless going to lots of trouble is how you work best; in that case, it's worth it.

It may take you some time to work out exactly how much character creation you have to do in advance. That will come with experience. Keep writing.

Things to remember

- Readers want to know if characters will be OK.
- Characters need to be capable, consistent and affected by the story's events.
- Characters in commercial erotic fiction are often beautiful, strong, vulnerable and passionate.
- The love interest and the antagonist might be the same person. Or there may be several of each.
- It's difficult to create character without plot, and vice versa.

Things to do

- Identify what you particularly like or dislike about a character when you're reading. Keep a note of these characteristics for future use.
- Make sure that your characters aren't perfect at the start of the story – they have to learn and to overcome their flaws.
- Identify the significant points of your main characters' backgrounds.

- Give characters names with meaning. The reader might not pick up on it, but you'll enjoy getting it right.
- Do as much character planning in advance as you need to, whether that's a little or a lot.

Where to next?

This chapter has focused on one side of the character/plot coin only. In Chapter 6 we'll be looking at plot in more detail, and this will have implications for the people in your stories.

6

A plot is a series of events that impact on characters' lives. In erotic fiction, the major story events involve sex, and the sex changes things.

Imagine a description of a sexual situation. For example, consider a blow-by-blow account of a couple engaged in light discipline. It's possible to describe the act in lots of sensory detail – the smell of the clean sheets, the thwack of palm on buttock, the heat rising from a rosy handprint. Four pages' worth of the whole thing from start to finish.

Now, this description could be very well written, and it may be sexually arousing. But a description of a sex act is not erotic fiction because there's no plot. Sex – even kinky sex – is just sex.

For the sex to be significant, it has to have impact on the characters involved. For that impact to become apparent to readers, we must have been introduced to the characters already and we need to understand what the lead character is looking for in this sexual encounter. Finally, we want to see how the characters' emotions and behaviour change as a result of the smacking session. Sex is the significant driver in erotic fiction, but it isn't everything.

You may find this chapter challenging, particularly if you haven't written a novel yet. We take it as slowly as we can. You should take your time, too. You might come back to it as you gain more writing experience.

Reasons to have sex

Why might a character have sex? Write down as many answers as you can imagine. Aim for 10, but keep going on to 20 or more, if possible.

- If you are struggling, consider people in different eras, or in vastly different circumstances from your own.
- Take a look at the categories of erotic fiction that we covered in Chapter 1. Why might characters in those different categories end up having sex? Add these reasons to your list.
- Your list will be a resource when you are creating plots. Keep it in a safe place and add to it as more reasons come to you. We're going to talk about the reasons for having sex later in this chapter.

Structure and the story outline

Tabitha Rayne, author

'Sex and the sexual/spiritual connection between my characters are always the most important elements within my books. However, the plot and story journey facilitate this connection.'

Aristotle was an ancient Greek philosopher, a teacher and a student of many subjects. Among other things, he wrote about theatre and poetry, the main literary forms of his day. He analysed successful plays and established how these stories satisfied their audiences. He reckoned that plot was the most significant element in spinning a tale, and he declared that each successful story had a beginning, a middle and an end.

Over the centuries, writers and theorists have either argued with Aristotle's conclusions or refined and adapted his ideas about plot structure. The structure of beginning, middle and end endures.

Not all stories are tightly plotted with a discernible pattern. Not all stories with a tight plot and discernible pattern are good examples of the craft. However, it's safe to say that the three-act structure – beginning, middle and end – works. Beginners don't need to worry about inventing something new.

Once you understand the three-act structure, you will recognize it everywhere: in stories you read, in film and television, and even in non-fiction. It is the scaffolding that holds scenes in the right place. It predicts the points in the story where things happen to change the storyline and to give shape to the plot. It's not the only configuration of scaffolding available, but it works.

We're not going to discuss the many variations of plot structure. We're concentrating solely on the ubiquitous three-act structure. Our explanation of it is has been influenced as much by screenwriting theory as fiction; some further sources of information are in the Appendix.

We think about the three-act structure in relation to the novel or novella, but it can be adapted for short stories, too.

The three-act structure

Act I is the beginning of the story. The reader is introduced to the story world and to the characters in it, and is given enough explanation about what's going on that she understands the impact of the changes to come in the lead character's life. It generally lasts for a quarter of the whole story.

Act II is the middle of the story where most of the action plays out. This act is usually twice the length of the others, so that it takes up half the text. The lead character deals with the changes wrought in Act I, learning about herself and the world as she faces the story's challenges. For ease of organization, in what follows we will divide the long Act II into two parts of equal length – Act IIa and Act IIb.

Act III is the end of the story. The lead character puts to use the knowledge she has gleaned in Act II, faces a final challenge and either succeeds in her endeavours or fails. It's a quarter of the story long. As the story progresses, it's likely that the pace will pick up, scenes becoming shorter, the timescale shrinking. For example, if Act I covers a week, then Act III lasts a day, or if Act I is an hour, Act III is a minute.

Things should get progressively worse for the lead character throughout the story. If you raise the tension and the action to its highest point in Act I, the only way is downhill. The reader would be seriously disappointed. Things have to be bad at the end of Act I, worse at the end of Act II and seemingly unbearable in Act III.

 Lily Harlem, author

'In pure erotica, a story about a sexual journey, readers (and some publishers) expect it to kick off with a smokin'-hot sex scene. This, of course, could be perceived as taking away your plot curve if you want sex to be the climax (excuse the pun) of the tale. However, the best way to achieve this is to have that first sex scene as something momentous, life-changing (or at least sex-life-changing) for your protagonist. That way, you can use the new emotions and stirred-up desires to fuel the rest of the story. An example could be someone watching their neighbours having sex and being so turned on by their first act of voyeurism that they set out on a journey to become the watched.'

Story outline and example story

Key scenes occur at specific points throughout the structure. By defining the roles of the key scenes and of the sections of story that link them together, we can create a high-level plan for the whole story. In this book, we concentrate on the story outline for a novel that has a happy ending (erotic fiction generally doesn't end in tragedy).

We've drafted an example story so that you can see how the story outline builds to a coherent plot.

Our first step was to identify the sexual issue at the heart of the story. We decided on a historical erotic novel set in the Dark Ages, about an English courtesan who is captured by Vikings and passed as a slave to their overlord back home. This idea appealed because the lead was sexually experienced and happy to regard her sexuality as a tool, and the love interest was big, hunky and a confirmed alpha male. So, by defining the sexual relationship, we identified who the story was about. A quick search on Saxon names threw up examples that we couldn't pronounce, so we made up the name Eda for the courtesan, and we called the love interest Leif.

Under each of the headings below, the first point defines the purpose of the scene or linking section, and the second illustrates this with Eda's story. Erotic fiction focuses on sex. So the key scenes usually have sexual content and involve the lead finding out more about her sexuality. The sex affects the story.

ACT I

Opening scene

The first scene shows the lead character in action, in her everyday world. She displays her major flaw, her significant virtue, and the motivation that will make her fight on.

Eda arrives haughty and disdainful in a provincial English village, ashamed that she's having to consort with the coarse village headman to pay her patron's gambling debts. The villagers don't know how to treat her – as a lady or as a whore. She's desperate to get this transaction over and done with so she can return to her daughter, who has been left in her patron's household in the city. Her flaw is arrogance, her virtue is bravery, and her motivation is to return to her daughter. The theme might be about debt and repayment.

Linking section 1

This section sets us up for what is to come. We receive enough information about the lead and her world so that we can understand the impact of the 'Inciting Incident' scene. This may be a short section.

Eda is disdainful of the headman's attempts to seduce her with little luxuries. It culminates in the unsatisfactory sexual transaction and the headman falling asleep and snoring loudly while she remains tied to his bed.

'Inciting Incident' scene

This scene is where something happens that changes the lead's world, for good, for ill, or as a mixed blessing. It throws her life into disarray. If it doesn't require much set-up, the Inciting Incident may take place in the opening scene.

Led by Harald (Leif's brother), the Vikings raid the village, killing everyone who stands against them, including the headman, and looting the headman's house. Eda tries to fight them off but they bind her in the headman's ropes and sling her on to a cart with other plunder.

Linking section 2

The lead identifies her goal to restore the equilibrium in her life that was destroyed by the Inciting Incident. This will drive her through the story. She tries to achieve her goal by taking the easiest possible steps. This doesn't work. She learns from her failures, and possibly from other people, that the problem will be harder to solve than she thought.

During the journey to the waiting Viking ship, Eda strikes out whenever they try to untie her. So they keep her bound and gagged. She endures the long sea voyage back to their homeland, fighting off their advances.

End of Act I scene

Something happens that changes the trajectory of the story. The lead finds out new information. Often, she will find herself in a new place, or a new social milieu, with lots to learn.

Eda is presented to Leif as a slave. He's physically impressive, and clearly intends to take sexual advantage of their respective positions, having

*heard about her hellcat reputation from Harald's men. Eda realizes that
there's no point in fighting him. And, even if he is a barbarian, he's a big
and hunky one. He carries her off to bed and asserts his ownership. She
can't prevent her physical reaction to him.*

ACT IIA

Linking section 3

The lead starts to learn about her new environment and to pick up
skills. She gets to know who her friends and enemies are. This is where
the story proper plays out, the events anticipated by the title and Act I.

*Eda has to earn a place in the homestead. She regards those around
her as barbarians, but gradually comes to appreciate their culture
and lifestyle. She gets to know another English slave, and gradually
changes her opinion of Leif. She mellows. She learns the language
and becomes a member of the Viking household.*

Midpoint scene

The middle of the story – this represents another major change in
the storyline. By now, the lead's new knowledge is coming in handy
and she decides upon a new course of action. She may bring the fight
to her enemy here, but she doesn't completely succeed over them yet.

*Eda returns to Leif's bed, with a very different attitude. They have
great sex. Eda thinks she's betraying herself, but she can't help it.*

ACT IIB

Linking section 4

Now the lead has a good idea of what she needs to do and of the
extent of the struggle ahead. However, more obstacles line up
against her, and her resolve falters.

*This starts with the honeymoon period during which there is lots
of sex and the start of an emotional commitment. By being around
Leif more, she comes to respect him as a leader and a man, and falls
in love. She finds out about the problems with a rival chief, Godred,
and his fearsome reputation. She meets Godred in Leif's company,
and it is clear that he desires her. She works out a plan to help Leif,
but he must be kept in the dark because he'd never endanger her.*

End of Act IIb scene

This seems the worst possible time, when she feels further than ever from achieving her goal. This scene is often marked by a death, or by the suggestion that death is a possible outcome. It is a false low point – the greatest battle is yet to come.

Eda escapes from the homestead, putting her plan to undermine Godred into action. She leaves a message with the fellow English slave. Eda presents herself at Godred's encampment. He thinks he's enticed Leif's beloved bed slave away. Some slightly twisted sex scene, here. This is the dark point for Eda; she's offered herself to a man she fears in defiance of the man she loves. She's isolated, worried about Leif and his people, disgusted by Godred, and frightened about what will happen when Godred tires of her. This is her lowest point. Despair all round. Then she finds out about Godred's one weakness. (We don't actually know what this is!)

ACT III

Linking section 5

The lead comes up with a possible solution to the problems that she now faces and starts to put it into action.

Eda escapes Godred's camp with the information that Leif needs. She reaches the village and throws herself on the mercy of Leif"s men, but an escaped slave is condemned to execution on sight. Before this can be carried out, one of the youngsters raises the general alarm, which brings everyone from the village running. Leif strides towards her. He grabs her by the hair, lifting her head to expose her throat to his blade and she manages to gasp out … something that stays his hand. Some word of warning? Leif listens. He realizes the value of the information, but wants her out of his sight and vows that she will be safely returned to England.

Decision point

The lead is faced with a dilemma and has to choose between two equally bad alternatives. The Decision Point may be in a scene of its own, or it may be part of the Climax scene.

Godred's attack is imminent. Eda can either escape now and return safely to her child, or stay and fight for the homestead. She decides to stay. She knows Godred can be defeated by his weakness (whatever that may be). She lets herself be recaptured by his men and taken back to his camp for punishment. Having run away twice, her punishment will be slow torture and death, unless Leif's forces win through and reach her in time.

Climax scene

The greatest battle. The lead puts into effect everything that she has learned throughout the story to confront the enemy and succeed. She brings about lasting change.

A grand battle takes place between Leif's forces and Godred's. Eda is being tortured by Godred as Leif leads his forces in an attack. Weakened though she is, Eda finds strength and manages to kill Godred with the knife that he was using to torture her, securing Leif's victory. She earns Leif's love and respect, but he has sworn to return her to her home. She must set out on the sea with Harald and his men.

Wrap-up key scene

This stands in opposition to the Opening scene and shows the changes in the lead, and the changes that the lead has wrought.

Leif can't watch her go. He abdicates his position as chief. Harald stays to run the homestead while Leif leads her homeward voyage. Dressed simply and elegantly, being handed into the ship by the man she loves, full of appreciation of the men around her and held high in their regard, Eda is a changed woman from the arrogant but debased courtesan of the opening scene.

The plan for Eda's story didn't all flow out in that order. We jumped around the story, coming up with ideas based on what we'd just decided. The story was worked out in the following order:

- Sexual issue – What's the heart of the story, and who are the lead and love interest?
- Inciting Incident – what causes all the problems?
- Climax – What's the final showdown, and how does the lead win the day?
- Wrap-up – What happens at the end, showing an HEA that might lead into another story?
- End of Act I – how does the lead find herself in a whole new world?
- Midpoint – What's the turning point of the whole story?

- End of Act IIb – What's the darkest moment, given the events of Act II and the coming Climax?
- Linking section 5 – What happens after the end of Act IIb, triggering the Climax?
- Decision – What dilemma must the lead face, determining how she will act in the Climax?
- Other linking sections – What are the logical steps between the other key scenes?
- Opening scene – Now that we know the whole story, what Opening scene would show us the character, her flaw, her virtue and her motivation?

This is an exercise to show you how a novel can be built from the first ideas to a story plan with a couple of hours' work. There are undeniably some gaps, but the structure could be developed until it's ready to be written.

In creating the plot, we created many primary, secondary and minor characters: Eda, Leif, Godred, Harald, the headman, the English villagers, the Viking crew, the Viking homesteaders, the English slaves, Godred's men, Harald's men, the slave rival who keeps the message (likely to have been set up earlier as a best friend character). We would now flesh out the primary and secondary characters using exercises from Chapter 5.

The three-act structure, expressed in the story outline, is just one way of building a story. The key scenes and linking sections break the expanse of a novel into manageable parts. If you think this structure might help you, there's no need to build a different one. If it hinders you, adapt or reject it, and do whatever is best for your story.

Analyse a story

- Identify a commercial story of any genre – a film or a novel – that you know very well indeed. This may not work so well with literary fiction or indie films.
- Note where the End of Act I, Midpoint and End of Act II scenes fall. They will be at points roughly a quarter, half, and three-quarters of the way through the story.
- Identify the remaining key scenes – Opening, Inciting Incident, Climax and Wrap-up.

The scene plan

The story outline must be expanded into somewhere between 60 and 120 scenes. The number of scenes depends on the complexity of the story (including the number of subplots) and the length of the book. Eda's story, as it currently stands, would probably work quite well as a novel of 80,000 words. That means there would be 20,000 words in each of Acts I, IIa, IIb and III. This translates into roughly 10 to 15 scenes per act. We'd aim for a total of 60 scenes for the whole novel.

Creating scenes for linking sections

The linking sections in the story plan need to be translated into scenes. Events must take place that allow the rest of the story to follow logically. In this exercise, you'll look at Linking section 3 in Act IIa.

The scenes must accomplish the following:
- Introduce all the characters we haven't met before, by the start of the midpoint at the latest.
- Show the growing relationship between Eda and Leif.
- Show the incremental change in Eda's emotions, from hellcat to a woman half in love.
- Show Eda becoming a member of the household.
- Show what happens to escaped slaves.
- Work in debt and repayment as the theme.

We have 15 scenes in Act IIa and we already know what happens in the last of those scenes.

You only have 14 scenes to do everything outlined above. Brainstorm story events (scenes) now.

More than one thing can happen in each scene. For example, Eda will need a bath. As a slave, she'll need someone to show her where to heat water and to point out the bathhouse, possibly the other English slave who will share the first few words of the new language. Eda will notice the well-appointed bathhouse, the pleasantly scented soap, the soft drying cloth. She starts to feel some respect for Viking culture. Then she might be shocked by the return of Leif's men with an escaped slave's head.

Create the 14 missing scenes and put them in the order that makes most sense to you.

About the example story

By making Eda a slave and Leif an insistent master, we have consent issues. In their first sex scene, Leif must expect sexual compliance, and Eda must clearly give it, knowing that she has no choice and regarding it as the best option. This is dub-con, or dubious consent.

In mainstream and popular erotic fiction, the lead and love interest often don't have other sexual partners once they've started an emotional relationship. Any sexual scene between Eda and Godred must be handled carefully, to make it clear that she's acting in Leif's best interests and that Godred is not an emotional rival. Even so, this may prove unpopular.

As Godred physically harms Eda during the torture scene, this would not be written as a fully erotic scene. Not *fully*. It's non-con, or non-consensual.

Eda has the point of view. Therefore, the things that happen in Leif's life can only be shown if Eda is also there.

An alternative structure would be to give Leif his own subplot, with certain scenes (not the key scenes) being told from his point of view. If so, he should have far fewer scenes than Eda, and they must be spread evenly throughout the story. This would also apply to any other character with a point of view – Godred would be a candidate for his own subplot, too. More subplots tend to make a story longer.

Now that we have a plan, we know what we must research: the time period, the geographies, clothing and housing on both sides of the sea, travel by longship, and so on.

Lucy Felthouse, author

'I think good plotting comes with practice. You may have an idea in your head that you think will make a brilliant novel, but when you get on with writing it, you may change your mind. It's important that your plot fits the length of what you're writing. For example, a very complex and involved plot is not going to work if you're writing a short story, and vice versa. The increasing demand for e-books means that we can pen stories without worrying too much about what their final word count will be.'

Long and short form

We've said before that erotic fiction has possibly the strongest market and reading public of any genre for short forms of fiction. And you already know that erotic novels and series have a potentially massive worldwide market. The short and long forms are defined by their word counts, but there are no official demarcations of length.

FLASH FICTION

Flash fiction is short, sometimes ultra short. You'll find online calls for submission for erotic flash fiction with defined word count limits. Generally, flash is up to 1,000 words, but can be as low as 100.

Many examples of erotic flash fiction can be found on authors' websites or blogs, so you can read widely and decide whether this is a form you'd like to try.

With flash, there's not enough room to get deeply into character, plot or setting. As with poetry, every single word has to count. You'll need an eye for the telling detail. Usually, flash concentrates on the moment during a sexual encounter when something changes; an adjustment of the power relationship between the lovers, the realization of erotic potential, a moment of insight. The key point about flash fiction is that, despite the restriction of words, the sexual act still needs to have some emotional underpinnings. Otherwise, as you know, it's porn.

Here's an excellent example of flash fiction, in 230 words:

'A Quiet Revolution' by Remittance Girl

In the bed's wasteland, I am set upon a mission.

Once he's shed his suit and his tie lies coiled like a dormant serpent on the floor, I engage him in the luxurious expenditure of his energies and, in doing so, deny the great machine its lifeblood.

He is unaware of my agenda. Caught up in the violence of his body's hunger, his hands have slipped the wheel of industry and settled on my thighs, my hips, my breasts. I've trapped his fingers in the tangled web of my long dark hair.

After his eyes have regained their focus. After I've supped on the warm excess that fountained from his cock to land on his thigh, he gazes at me in hazy lassitude.

'I bet I can make you come again,' I say.

He smiles. 'You think?'

'I do,' I say. 'Especially if I do this ...'

The tip of my tongue chases sensation up the underside of his semi-erect shaft. My lips purse and suck-kiss the vulnerable spot that nestles beneath the head. Then, in an act of understated warfare, I cover him with my mouth and trap him in the vacuum of my intentions.

Every unit of energy I take from him denies the machine. Every thrust, every breathy gasp, every tense shuddering is an act of sabotage. It's a very quiet, very underhanded sort of revolution.

SHORT STORIES

The thriving erotic short-story market seeks work that ranges from around 1,000 words to, very occasionally, 20,000 words. Anthologies tend to look for 5,000 to 6,000 words. If you are submitting work, meet the organizer's maximum length requirements. There are many examples of free erotic short stories available online.

We recommend the short form for new writers. It's possible to complete short stories quickly and move on to the next one. They give you lots of experience of shaping plots, creating characters and improving your writing. They're easier to handle than novellas and novels, and you're less likely to get lost. There's usually not enough space for a large cast – confine your attention to the main players only. The short story may focus on just one sex session.

In writing a short story, your plot may need to identify only the beginning, middle and end, but you can use the story structure template for further guidance within these broad headings. Sometimes the entire short story will take place within one scene, sometimes more. It's worth setting up the characters, the situation they find themselves in, and the setting carefully. Remember to trace the emotional impact of the action on the lead. For her, something will change. The change may be subtle, or might not be expected to last very long. That's all you can expect to be credible over so few words. But make sure change is in there.

NOVELLAS

Works between 7,000 and 60,000 words are known as novellas, with the shorter versions of around 7,000 to 17,000 words sometimes being called novelettes. Novellas might have just one very long scene or go up to around 30 scenes. Stand-alone novellas are available, particularly in electronic formats, as are novellas that flesh out the stories of characters in existing novels and series, providing extra material for fans. Themed collections of three or so erotic novellas in one volume are popular.

In comparison with short stories, the writer spends more time on establishing the plot, characters and locations, potentially as much as for a novel. There's room for a few more characters and scope to explore more than one sexual encounter. A typical structure would be to open a novella with one sex scene that's hot but not mind-blowing (such as a scene that doesn't involve the love interest), then go on to a second, 'better' sex scene in the middle with the new lover, and a final explosive sex scene when the main characters have the measure of each other.

In comparison with a full novel, the novella can be regarded as the lead and love interest's relationship storyline with all of the peripherals and subplots taken out. They're often about establishing and improving a sexual and emotional relationship, with plenty of scope for character impact and change.

NOVELS

From around 60,000 to 120,000 words or more in length, novels tend to have between 40 to 100-plus scenes. A length of more than 120,000 words is unusual in erotic fiction.

The novel's length gives scope to include additional characters, settings and subplots alongside the main storyline. Subplots are other stories running alongside the lead's story, such as separate issues affecting the lead's life, or stories centred on other POV characters and showing events when the lead may not be present. Subplots also have a beginning, middle and end, and can be planned with key scenes using the story structure. It's possible that not all subplot scenes are shown in the novel – they may be referred to, or assumed, or be accepted knowledge in the story world.

Common novel storylines concern the varied sexual adventures of the lead character and what she learns about herself and the world along the way, or the establishment of a sexual and often romantic relationship against the odds.

Novels might be published in parts as serials, and there's been a recent surge in interest for erotic serials available electronically. Series of novels are several novels with plots that are complete in themselves, but which share elements such as characters or story worlds. These are hugely popular with readers who eagerly await the next release, keen to find out more about favourite characters. In developing series, writers plant the seeds of up-and-coming storylines in earlier books.

 Know the form

Which of the forms – flash, short story, novella or novel – do you have least knowledge of? Make a point of allocating some research time to finding and reading good examples of the form. Examples from established publishers will tend to be of more consistent quality.

Sex and conflict

Conflict is essential in fiction. First, it makes the lead's goal hard to achieve, so there has to be a whole story's worth of action while she tries to win the day. Second, it makes the reader worry.

In the best genre fiction, the reader worries about how the lead is going to deal with the challenge on this page, and she worries about what on earth is going to happen next. She knows that things will only get worse for the lead as the plot progresses (so you'd better make them worse). Worry creates tension. Tension keeps her turning pages.

Make sure that you have conflict or tension in every single scene. If you find a scene with no tension or conflict, write some into it. If there are two people in the scene, make them want different things, or the same thing but only one of them can get it, or get them into an argument. It's better if the conflict and tension are related to your storyline, but any tension is better than none. When positive things happen to your characters, they should happen in spite of or as a result of all the bad things that are going on around them.

At the start of this chapter, there was an exercise about reasons for having sex. Did you get 10 reasons, or 20? Here's our list:

- To have children
- As an expression of love
- For lust
- To gain comfort or companionship
- For recreation
- As a slave's duty
- As a master's right
- As a monarch's duty
- In return for money or another payment
- As a payment or bribe
- In exchange for a favour
- To get close to an enemy
- As an act of worship
- As part of a religious rite
- To make someone else envious
- To seek favour for another
- To offer consolation
- To consolidate a disguise
- Out of curiosity
- In accepting punishment
- To punish
- To make amends
- To gain information
- To gain distance from a previous lover
- As instructed by a figure in authority
- As part of an experiment
- As a performance

- To help the partner forget
- Compelled by hypnosis or drugs
- As a promise of a future relationship
- To try out a potential partner
- To keep up with peers
- To induct a novice
- To learn as a novice
- As a bet or dare
- As an act of rebellion
- Through naivety
- Out of pity
- For old times' sake
- As a case of mistaken identity
- For revenge

We're sure that there must be many that we've missed. Like you, we'll add to our list over time.

The main driver of story is conflict. No conflict, no story. People generally don't want to read about characters with blessed lives. You might write a piece without any conflict, but it won't be a proper story.

Story Seeds From Sex

Look at your list of reasons for having sex, and add any that you like from our list.

- Can you think of ways that the individual reasons could either be the result of conflict, or could lead to conflict? Exercise your storytelling muscles.
- Which reason interests you most? Use this as the seed for a story, and have a go at developing a story structure.
- If this is working for you, try a scene plan. If it isn't, put it aside and come back to it another time. Your mind will probably ponder on it and come up with a story when you're not looking.
- You may even want to write the story.

For good erotic fiction, both sex and conflict are essential, and either one could lead to the other: sex arises from conflict, or sex leads to conflict by getting in the way of the character's goals.

Even sex as an expression of love must create conflict. To fall in love might be the very worst thing that could happen to your lead and love interest (they already have partners; it interferes with their role or job; they're from warring clans, etc.) or the sex could place them in danger (of being caught, of falling ill, of betraying their whereabouts, and so on).

Depending on the way you've set up the story, and on the story's length, characters will have both a story problem and a sexual problem. These are usually linked. Eda's story problem is that she's a captive overseas. Her sexual problem is that she must have sex with Leif as a slave's duty.

Problems, goals and motivation

When you're creating a story, you need to know what problem your lead is facing, what her goal is, and why she wants that. Her problem relates to what's happened to her world in the Inciting Incident key scene. Her goal is what she wants to do about it. Why she wants to achieve the goal is her motivation, the reason she keeps trying rather than walking away from the challenge.

If your character's problem is that she's horny and her only goal is to get laid, guess what? Porn alert! By the rule of no-conflict-no-story, sex is the very last thing she can get, and it'll arrive in the Wrap-up scene, if at all. Certainly, your character can want to have sex, and can intend to have sex, but there needs to be a problem standing in the way of getting it, something she'll formulate a new goal to deal with. She wants to have sex … but she doesn't have a partner and she's too shy to pick anyone up … but she's sneaking out of the house at eleven and must be home by midnight … but she's promised him anal and now she's nervous. These problems are the right size for a scene or a short story. Novel-sized problems would be harder to solve; they require more action and bigger changes from the lead.

The reader needs to know the lead's story goal early on. It's easier for the reader to follow if the goal is expressed concretely; you should be able to take a photograph of the lead achieving it. So, rather than the abstract 'find happiness', her heart's desire might be to wake up every morning between the hot twins who live next door. Instead of 'making him pay', she'll want to hear the jury deliver a guilty verdict. Remember that different characters would respond to the same problem by coming up with different goals, dependent upon their personality. To a different character, 'making him pay' might mean cutting his lying tongue out. Goals can be given urgency by the ticking clock – time is running out, and the pace becomes frantic.

Motivation is what drives the character to take action to achieve her goal without giving up, in spite of all the conflict that you're going to throw in her path. She has to have a good reason for putting herself on the line, particularly if her behaviour deviates from her normal pattern. Why is this time different? Why doesn't she just go home and forget about it? Without strong and appropriate motivation, characters lose credibility. When we outlined Eda's story, we started with the problem that she'd been abducted by Vikings, and her goal was to return home. Her motivation was that she needed to get back to her daughter. If you pick the right motivation for the lead's goal, readers will empathize.

The other major characters have problems, goals and motivations, too. These will be contrary to the lead's goals, leading to conflict. If the antagonist succeeds, the lead must fail, and vice versa.

OBSTACLES

There are five levels of obstacle that can stand in the way of your character achieving her goals.

1 Personal obstacles set the character at war with herself. Something in her psychological or physical make-up is stopping her from achieving her goal – she wants to be a stripper but she's scared she'll look foolish.

2 Interpersonal obstacles lie between the character and someone else. There's one strip joint in town, and it's run by her arch-enemy from high school.

3 Societal obstacles means that some impersonal rule or institution is stopping the character. She'd be ostracized and lose her job as a primary school teacher if anyone got wind of her extreme fan dance.

4 Natural obstacles pit the character against a powerful non-human force. She's landed a gig, stripping for a stag night in the private room of a bar across town, but the storm has closed the only bridge over the river.

5 Supernatural obstacles set the character against the divine. She's worried that stripping offends the goddess (as if), but she's got to raise money somehow to pay for little Jimmy's medicine. Tonight.

Don't hesitate to pile on the misery for your characters; use obstacles from more than one level at the same time. Stories work best when the lead is challenged on more than one level. The lead will probably have both an external and an internal goal.

Eda's external goal is to return home. Her internal goal might be to find Mr Right, but she falls in love with her Viking master. Now she's both physically enslaved far across the sea (external societal and natural obstacles) and emotionally tied (internal personal obstacle).

AT THE SCENE LEVEL

Problems, goals, motivation, obstacles and conflict come into play at both the story level and the scene level.

For example, in Eda's sex scene with the headman, her problem is she has to service this distasteful man, her goal is to get it over and done with quickly, her motivation is that she can get away from the village sooner, and the conflict comes from the headman who leaves her tied up – an interpersonal obstacle.

Is Eda the kind of character who will put up with being tied up? Or will she fight it? The answer to this will both illuminate her character and determine the action of the rest of the scene. Because this is the Inciting Incident, it will in turn influence the rest of the story. Remember that, when the scene takes place, Eda's an experienced courtesan who has no reason to be afraid.

SETTING AND CONFLICT

Depending upon your story, you may need to create a setting consisting of one room, or an alternative universe where the laws of physics are different, or anything in between.

- What are the geographical and temporal aspects of the setting? What is life like for people in that place at that time? What are the general causes of conflict in that society?
- What's keeping the characters there? If things are getting tough for the characters on every page, what's to stop them leaving? Perhaps they physically can't get away: for example they're stranded on a desert island, or in prison, or on a cruise ship. Perhaps something that they value has been put at risk. Again, depending on your story, the thing at risk could be a relationship, the lead's self-esteem, or life as we know it.

- What difference is the setting making to the characters? Are the characters comfortable in the setting, so they're more relaxed and open to suggestion than they might be? Or are they uncomfortable, creating more scope for tension and conflict?
- What difference are the characters making to the setting? Are they altering the setting physically, or are they finding a cure for the common cold, or are they ushering in a new social order? Or are they trying to leave it completely unchanged?
- Use as few different settings as possible in a story. Let the reader get to know the story's places, and let those places become meaningful to the reader and the characters over several scenes.

Outline your story

Complete the following outline for a short story. Start anywhere you like in the structure.

Overall

- What reason for having sex are you going to write about? Does it cause conflict or arise from conflict?
- Who are the lead and love interest characters? Any others?
- What are the lead's external and internal problems?
- What are the lead's goal and motivation?
- What are the love interest's problem, goal and motivation?

Act I

- How does the story open?
- What's the inciting incident?
- What happens next?
- What has changed at the End of Act I?

Act IIa

- What happens next?
- What surprise comes at the middle of the story?

Act IIb

- What happens next?
- What is the worst thing that could happen to the lead?

Act III
- What happens next?
- What decision does the lead have to make?
- What's the final climactic struggle?
- What has changed?

Refine the outline until you're happy with all your choices.

Carry out any research that you need and make notes.

Write. Aim for 3,000 words.

The three-act structure is worth getting to know even if you are resistant to planning in advance. When you come out of your writing frenzy, you'll either be stuck in the middle of your story with no idea what to do next, or you'll have a massive pile of paper that you need to wrestle into shape. The three-act structure will be your guide.

Focus points

If plot feels like a massive, complicated issue, use the three-act structure as scaffolding. You can start playing with different story shapes later.

Things to remember

- The three-act structure of beginning, middle and end has stood the test of time.
- Things must get progressively worse for the lead throughout the story.
- In creating plots, we also create characters.
- A story outline tells you what you need to research.
- When planners have a scene plan, they can start to write. When non-planners have a scene plan, they can start to revise.
- Each scene may have to accomplish several things, moving the story on and setting up events to come.
- In erotic fiction, sex either causes conflict or is caused by conflict.

Things to do

- Look out for the three-act structure in any story you come across, whatever the medium.
- Use the seven key scenes and the five linking sections to structure your plot.
- Don't settle for the first reason that comes to mind for a sex scene.
- Establish your primary characters' problems, goals and motivations.
- For each scene, work out the POV character's problem, goal, obstacle, conflict and motivation.
- Build conflict into the setting – for both characters and plot.

Where to next?

This is the last of three chapters about storytelling skills. Next, we look at wordcraft – the skills that you'll use in expressing yourself on the page. First, we take a general view of these skills in Chapter 7 – Writing well.

7

Writing well

In Chapters 1 to 3 we discussed the creativity and self-management skills that writers need, so that they know where and how to start. In Chapters 4 to 7 we concentrated on storytelling skills – ways of taking your good, creative ideas and developing them until they are ready to be realized on the page.

In this chapter and the following two, we will look at the final skill set relating to writing fiction, namely the skills of wordcraft, or writing well. Wordcraft determines whether the writer will be able to make the most of the stories that she has developed.

Those involved in publishing erotic fiction say that there's more erotic content available now than ever before. But there's general agreement that, while there are some outstanding stories, much of what's available isn't very good. It offers only tired ideas, derivative plots or implausible characters. The most successful erotic fiction of all time prompted a battalion of critics to write scathing reviews in the press and online. Much of that criticism targeted that novel's wordcraft.

Critics are a great source of information. Make time to read erotic fiction book reviews; they point out what's good and bad, what works and what doesn't. Read the book and see if you agree. If those in the know criticize an aspect of writing, it's worth paying attention. Somewhere on the page, the writer has made the kind of mistake that we want to recognize and avoid.

For millions of readers worldwide, the standard of writing didn't stop them devouring the *Fifty Shades* series. There was a real thrill of discovery in the air. Let's welcome the new readership to our genre and offer them quality as well as quantity.

 ## Edit exercise

- Read the 'Two People Meet' story that you wrote at the start of Chapter 4. (If you didn't do this exercise, use any other piece of erotic fiction that you have written.)
- What do you think of it now?
- Before you go on to read this chapter, change anything that needs to be changed. Do you need to give more information? Should you cut parts of it? Is there anything you've learned that you'd like to incorporate?
- What's good about this piece of work?
- How do you think it compares with other writers' published stories?

Basic principles

 ## Lily Harlem, author

'Understand the art of creative writing. You've got to have the basics sorted because there are some amazingly talented people out there writing incredible books. If you start head-hopping, using clichés, or allowing your characters to have independent body parts ("my hand moved down his back", as opposed to "I moved my hand down his back"), your book will stand out as unprofessional and won't be pleasant to read.

> *Writing erotic fiction is hard – it's one physical act retold a million times, and you need to be able to tell it in a million different ways.'*

In the best genre writing, the reader's gaze flows over the words on the page, images form effortlessly in her mind, and the story is delivered straight to her imagination. When beginning writers are unhappy with their first attempts at fiction, they might not be able to pinpoint what's wrong. They just know that their story doesn't flow like the stories in books.

In contrast with genre, literary fiction sometimes does call the reader's attention to the writing, slowing her down so that she can admire the beautiful prose. This control is not the same as making beginners' mistakes.

Whether you hope to write popular and commercially successful genre or serious and critically acclaimed literature, it's worth learning the principles of writing well. You'll find published examples of writers who get by without adhering to these principles. But we want your writing to be the best.

Warning – if you have little writing experience, some of these principles may be beyond your understanding at the moment. Concentrate on mastering principles 1 to 7 first.

1 KEEP YOUR OWN VOICE

Your writing voice should be similar to your speaking voice. Imagine you're telling the story to an interested friend. Don't try to sound clever or grand or quirky – you will come across as pompous or affected, and you're more likely to make mistakes, such as using words wrongly.

If you're struggling with how to set something down on the page, perhaps you've lost track of your own voice. Ask yourself out loud 'What am I trying to say?' and then answer yourself out loud. Listen to the words you use – is that really what you're trying to say? Keep talking to yourself until you've got it right, then put that on the page.

2 PUNCTUATE PROPERLY

Much of the erotic fiction available online hasn't been professionally edited. We've seen some crazy disregard for the conventions of writing. For example, we found a short story a good few thousand words long with no paragraphing, just one block of text. We couldn't face reading it. Make it easy for the reader; use sentences and paragraphs, and keep punctuation simple.

- Use full stops at the end of sentences.
- Whole novels can be punctuated using only full stops, commas and inverted commas (speech marks).
- Exclamation marks may be used sparingly, and only in thoughts or dialogue.
- Only use colons and semicolons if you know what you're doing, and never in dialogue.
- Ellipses ('…') mean that the thought or the dialogue has trailed off.
- Dashes at the end of dialogue ('Please, just put it —') show that the speech has been interrupted.
- AVOID block and Spurious Capitals because they're Annoyingly CHILDISH. And so are *italics* if they're used for *emphasis*. Do not even go there with underlining. Use sentence structure to give emphasis in your writing, not font. Trust your reader. (See principle 14, 'Make the most of power positions', below.)
- Change paragraph as often as you need to. Paragraphs have one or more sentences about a particular topic. A new topic needs a new paragraph. In fiction, this can be a matter of style; you will develop your own. But look at any published piece of fiction and work out why the writer decided to paragraph where she did.
- A double space between paragraphs means one of two things in fiction: either a chunk of time has passed between the two paragraphs, or there's a change in viewpoint character. Don't automatically double-space between paragraphs just because that's what you do in business writing. You're a fiction writer now.

For your first steps in erotic fiction, stick with the tried and tested. If you can't find what you're trying to do in printed books, that's because publishers believe it won't work for the general reader. Their business depends on getting this right. Once you've mastered the conventions, you can experiment as much as you like.

3 BE PRECISE

We're putting images in the reader's brain and we want the images to be sharp. We achieve this with precise language, particularly nouns and verbs. Don't say 'pet' when you mean 'Chihuahua'. Don't settle for 'went' when your character 'sauntered'.

Edit exercise

- Look again at your 'Two People Meet' story. Go through it, underlining all the verbs and circling all the nouns and noun phrases. Actually do this on the page. Have you been as precise in these as you need to be? Is there a better word?

4 EXERCISE RESTRAINT

Some things that are drilled into us at school in English lessons are wrong for creative writing:

- **Varying words.** While you don't want to overuse words, it's also true that you don't need to think up a new term for something every time you mention it. You can talk about a cock repeatedly, so there's no need to call it a love muscle. Or similar.

- **Said.** In fiction, 'said' is like punctuation. It's there to help with meaning. The reader doesn't 'see' it, so there is no need to change it to whispered, yelled, exclaimed, and so on. 'Said' tells the reader who is talking, and it may be used to improve the rhythm of a dialogue exchange. In a conversation between two people, you won't have to use it very often – the reader will follow the exchange until there's a pause. After that, you may need to use it again to identify the speaker. And notice that 'said' always comes after the person's name or their pronoun, as in 'Jane said' or 'he said'. The other way round, 'said Jane', is like a children's book, and 'said he' smacks of Victorian poetry. After a question in dialogue, you can use 'asked'.

- **Adverbs.** Some writers use them; some think they're best avoided. We'd avoid them where possible. Adverbs often show that you've not been precise in your choice of verb. Compare 'he walked slowly' with 'he strolled'. In dialogue attributions, such as 'she said sarcastically', write the line of dialogue so that the sarcasm is apparent, and trust the reader to pick up on it.

- **Adjectives.** Limit yourself to one per sentence (a completely arbitrary limit, but you get the idea). There's a danger in erotic fiction that you'll slip into purple prose – overblown, ornate language with too much sensory detail. It makes the reader snigger. Control yourself.

- **Similes.** These regularly degenerate into clichés, especially when used in a sex scene. You know the type: 'as thick as a …', 'as hot as a …', 'as long as a …'. If you must use them, be sure that the comparison is really needed to help the reader visualize the scene, and that you've never seen that particular simile used before.
- **Sentence structure.** Although you can craft long and complex sentences that are grammatically correct, you don't want the flow of images to stop while the reader tries to follow your syntax. Make it easy for her by using simple sentence constructions. That's not to say that there's no place for complex sentences in erotic fiction; just remember that your job is to entertain the reader, not lose her.

5 VARY SENTENCE LENGTH

It's easy to slip into a pattern of sentence length. You don't notice you've done it. You see it when you read back through your work. It's likely that you'll find the paragraph monotonous. Your mind may start to wander. You need to change the sentence length. Like this. And you've probably noticed that 'like this' is actually a fragment rather than a whole sentence; these are allowed nowadays, as are sentences that start with 'and', 'but' or 'so'.

6 CRAFT YOUR DIALOGUE

Dialogue is not natural speech put down on the page. In natural speech, we might change tense, mess with grammar, hesitate, contradict ourselves, pause, and use space holders like 'erm' and 'uh' while we gather our thoughts. Human interaction is eased by inconsequential small talk. Not in dialogue.

Dialogue tries to reproduce the natural rhythms of speech while cutting out meaningless rubbish. It may be part of a character's reaction to an event ('Don't worry, darling. It happens to everyone.'), or their attempt to elicit a suitable reaction from another character ('Harder!'). Here are five ways to improve dialogue.

1 **Understand how dialogue is laid out on the page:**
   - Every time someone new takes a turn to speak, start a new paragraph.
   - Use speech marks around everything that's said, including the punctuation.

- When a line of dialogue is being attributed, use a comma before the closing speech mark and single space after it: *'I can't keep my hands off you,'* he said.
- If it's not being attributed, use a full stop: *'You're irresistible.'*
- If it's a question, use the question mark whether it's being attributed or not. If it is attributed, use a single space after the speech marks and no following capital letter: *'Can you do it again?'* she asked.
- If a question is not attributed, start the next sentence as you would normally: *'You want to put it where?'* His eyes watered.
- If there's a short pause in the dialogue while the person talking does something or thinks, or while you mention what's happening apart from the dialogue, there doesn't need to be a new paragraph when she talks again – she retains the dialogue.
- If there's a longer pause with paragraph changes between two lines of dialogue, the next time someone speaks, give them a new paragraph.

If you're unsure about any of this, look at professionally published fiction for guidance.

2 Use character-specific words and ways of speaking.

Your character will have words that she uses, and things that she'd never say. And everyone switches between different ways of speaking to suit the situation, for example at the pitch side compared with in the boardroom. Match the type of speech to the speaker and the situation.

In erotic fiction, this will include the character's preferred words for genitals and for sexual acts. While word choice is partly driven by sub-genre or heat rating, it will also reflect character.

3 Cut small talk.

Unless there's something significant going on, go straight to the point of the conversation. The reader won't miss the hi-how-are-you bits. You can also cut explicit agreement, because the reader will assume it's been made. For example, if one character asks, 'Can I come in?' and the response is 'Excuse the mess,' we know that the second character has agreed.

4 Notice what people miss out in speech.
   • They contract words: *'She's mine.'*
   • They miss words altogether: *'Got to go.'*
   • They use someone's name or designation only once to catch their attention, then probably won't use it again (unless it's to show respect to an authority figure, in which case they'll use it every time they speak, ma'am.).
   • Missing out parts of speech makes dialogue seem more natural.

5 Play with subtext.

   Readers interpret what they read. Scenes come to life when the reader picks up on the subtext – the things that the characters are not saying. While the surface conversation might be about who's turn it is to put the bins out, what's really going on is a negotiation over foreplay.
   • In particular, readers enjoy interpreting the dialogue of the non-POV character, looking for subtext about the relationship between the two main characters.
   • Subtext can be apparent in actions as well as words.
   • As you plan a scene, decide what your subtext is going to be about, but have your characters talk about something else.

6 Have a very light touch with accents or dialects.

   Accents that have been spelled out phonetically are difficult to read and can be patronizing or offensive.
   • It's possible to convey some accents and dialects by means of word choice (petrol vs. gas) and by speech patterns ('Sure it's a beautiful day.').
   • Don't overdo it. Your lead will notice an unusual accent, so the reader will pick it up from the lead's thoughts. Many stories don't mention accents at all.
   • And be aware of dialect translation difficulties. American English has different definitions of some British English words – be careful with pants and fannies.

Lily Harlem, writer

'A lot of authors forget one of the best tools when writing a sex scene, and that's dialogue. Sex talk, dirty talk, is hot in real life and it's hot on the page, too. Not just 'Oh' and 'Ah,' but actual conversation. You can use longer sentences when it's a prolonged foreplay and then make them short and snappy to project urgency, the cresting of orgasm, as the finale approaches. Use this sentence structure technique in some of the prose, too; it works really well.'

7 SHOW, DON'T TELL

'Show, don't tell' is one of the better-known principles of creative writing.

We're telling when we summarize. Chapter 4 opened with an exercise based on 'two people meet and have sex'. That phrase is a summary. Lots of things must have happened to the characters, time must have passed, but it's all been condensed into six words that take a second to read.

There is no way that the reader's emotions can be engaged by that six-word summary of a story. If the sex scenes are important, it's essential that you don't summarize sex. We don't need every thrust described – too much detail – but we do want to enjoy the significant events in all their glory. A poor attempt at engaging the reader included the immortal line 'I gave him a blow job.' Turned on? No.

In the Chapter 4 'Two People Meet' exercise, you thought about the bits of story that you wanted to show, to turn into scenes. First sight, first meeting, first kiss. Writers create a blow-by-blow account of the events that prompt emotion, and hence action, in our characters. This creates reaction and feelings in our readers. If your story says that 'He looked really hot and it turned her on', your reader can understand it, she might accept it's true, but she can't feel it. If she felt it, she'd know it was true. You need to spell out what makes him hot, and how she knows she's turned on. Give her enough detail so that she can screen the story in her mind. Show her.

However, telling is good for the bits that you need to include for logic's sake, but that are too boring to show. This includes day-to-day life that doesn't affect the story ('she made dinner'), and anything that the reader already knows about. For example, you could summarize a character's account of a previous scene by saying 'She told Lily what had happened.'

Another way of thinking about 'show, don't tell' is that we avoid using abstract terms. You might want to write about equality, loyalty, fun or slavery. You can only do this in story by turning them into concrete events, with characters reacting and experiencing emotional states.

Edit exercise

- Abstract terms include naming emotions. In your 'Two People Meet' story, can you find a point where you have summarized an emotion? Look out for things like 'he was nervous,' or 'I was turned on'. How would you would show that emotion rather than telling it? Think about what you felt in that situation, what you thought, how you handled it. Showing takes a lot longer than telling.

8 FILTER THROUGH POINT OF VIEW

In scenes, everything is experienced through a character's point of view. If she knows that the thing on the table is a gimp mask, you can use those words. If she doesn't know, she'll describe it more generally. This modifies our advice to be precise: be precise as far as your POV character's knowledge allows.

Using your POV character as a filter helps you present information in the right order. She will take in the bigger aspects of the setting first before zooming in on the finer details; she'll register the warm candlelight before she notices the cuffs on the headboard. She'll notice novel sensations before the familiar: the cold steel around her wrists before the cotton sheet against her cheek.

Use the POV character's mood or emotional state to filter detail – you don't need to describe everything. In a crowded bar, a nervous character will notice different details compared with a character who's horny. Identify the POV character's emotional state at the start of a scene and be aware of when it changes.

9 USE FILTERS WHEN DESCRIBING CHARACTERS

Your characters will describe things as they see them. Your lead's point-of-view filter is always at work, even when she observes herself. You can drip-feed your reader with details of your lead character's appearance. They will pick up on clues such as the fact that she needs to tie her hair back before scrubbing the hearth, or that he needs to shave again before he goes out to the ball. Let the details slip out naturally in the course of the story. Don't have your lead stand in front of the mirror wondering 'Am I too thin? Does my tumbling, tawny hair need trimming?' And if her livelihood depends on her looks or physique, she'll be more interested in maintenance than self-admiration.

Readers are happy to wait to see what other characters think of the lead's looks.

The love interest, on the other hand, can be described in as much admiring detail as you like, all through the lead's filter. It's best drip-fed rather than delivered as a chunk of description. The lead will find the love interest physically attractive early in their relationship, usually from their first meeting and in spite of any conflicts or mixed feelings. Use her changing emotional state to control how and when descriptive details are released. In this way, we learn both about the love interest's looks and the lead's state of mind.

Especially in longer fiction, whatever your lead finds exceptionally attractive about your love interest is worth repeating in as many scenes as you can.

10 GIVE MORE PAGE TIME TO IMPORTANT CHARACTERS

When the relationship between the lead and the love interest is developing, describe every single thing that happens. Give us a detailed build-up to their scenes together. Pay attention to the minutiae of both verbal and non-verbal communication, the kind of thing that we'd obsessively analyse in real life. Keep the pair in the scenes together until the whole thing is played out. Make sure that each scene they have together either creates or shows a change in their relationship. Give us the lead's reaction to what happened, and the love interest's, too, if you've structured your story to allow this.

When the lead is with other characters, don't go into all that detail. The best advice is to 'get in late, get out early'. That means, start the scene as close to the main action as you can, and leave the scene as soon as possible after the scene's action has produced some change in the POV character. The amount of page time that you give to characters indicates their importance in the story. If a secondary character is taking over your story, cut their page time.

11 MAINTAIN POINT OF VIEW

We mentioned in Chapter 4 that you should keep to the same POV character within a scene, and not go bouncing around in different people's heads (unless you are being truly omniscient and/or mildly experimental, and we wouldn't recommend either of these for beginners). For new writers, the best time to shift POV is between scenes.

In a long, key scene, you might think about changing the POV halfway through, so the reader can access the other character's thoughts and feelings. However, you can only do this if you've set up a pattern of changing POV in the rest of the story.

12 VARY DISTANCE

Film uses a variety of shots, from wide establishing shots to extreme close-up. Similarly, a story will take us from the overall scene of the beach party in full swing, to a focus on a girl in a bikini dancing like she doesn't care, to a close-up on the waiter's fingertips brushing across the seat of her bikini bottoms as he walks past.

Distance in fiction also relates to how deep into a character's mind the writer allows us to go:

- *Brad watched her dance. He thought that she had the perfect ass.* 'He thought' keeps us at a distance from the POV character.

- *Brad watched her dance. She had the perfect ass.* Taking out 'He thought that', we can still tell that Brad is doing the thinking. We're closer to his actual thoughts.

- *Brad watched her dance. God, that perfect ass.* Now we are closest of all, directly experiencing what Brad is thinking in his own words, and he's not thinking in sentences.

Given the need for emotional content in erotic fiction, the deeper we can go into characters' thoughts at key moments, the better. Most stories vary the distance, coming in to extreme close-up and moving out again to wider shots throughout the story. If you don't want the reader to know what's going on in the POV character's thoughts, come right up out of her head and stick to objective details.

Further principles

Once you've mastered the points above, it's time to get a bit more technical:

13 USE ACTIVE LANGUAGE WHEN IT MAKES SENSE

Writers are often urged to use the active voice as it is more engaging for the reader. In passive language, 'The bouquet was sent by Adam.' In active language, 'Adam sent the bouquet.' However, the passive also has its merits, particularly for emphasis (see 'Make the most of power positions' below) when you want to hold back the interesting piece of information until the end of the sentence.

Use the active voice in general but, if the passive voice is better for a particular sentence, do what's best for your writing.

14 MAKE THE MOST OF POWER POSITIONS

If you are not going to use italics to add emphasis, what can you use? In that sentence, the astute reader knows that the emphasis in the last clause is on 'can' because she interprets the context. However, there are power positions at the end of sentences, stronger ones at the end of paragraphs, and strongest of all at the ends of chapters. Consider the difference between the following two sentences:

He found a dildo under her pillow.

Under her pillow, he found a dildo.

The second sentence has more of a 'ta-dah!' ring to it. We wonder what he's going to find, then it's revealed.

Under her pillow, he found a dildo and he wondered how long it had been there.

Do you really want to bury the dildo's ta-dah under another clause? Is 'there' a worthy holder of the power position? Be careful not to fritter them away.

Check out the ends of sentences and paragraphs in your emotional memory story. Do you need to rearrange the words to make the most of the power positions?

15 AVOID MELODRAMA

Characters' emotional reactions to the things that are going wrong must be proportionate to whatever has just happened to them. If characters over-react, or if the cause of their reaction is unclear, we have melodrama. With erotic fiction's need for emotional impact, be aware of the danger of losing proportionality.

16 WRITE WHAT DOES HAPPEN,
NOT WHAT DOESN'T

Positives in fiction are easier to read and follow than negatives. If you phrase things negatively, the reader has to imagine the positive first, then take it away. An accumulation of negatives in fiction can be wearing.

She hadn't reached the bedroom before he pounced.

She had reached the hall when he pounced.

He wore nothing except his bow tie.

He wore only his bow tie.

Some writers may find this too subtle to worry about, but we think it subliminally affects the story's tone and the reader's comfort.

17 MAINTAIN POINT OF VIEW AGAIN

It can be difficult to completely expunge POV drift from your work. There are two occasions when you have to be particularly careful, because the drift is very subtle:

- **When the POV character is describing herself.** You can't say that your POV character 'gave an enigmatic smile', for example, because she knows why she's smiling. It would have to be an external judgement that her smile's enigmatic. She could intend it to be enigmatic, or someone could comment that it is so, but you need to say that explicitly on the page.
- **When you're describing a non-POV character's reactions.** You can't say 'he shrugged in confusion', because your POV character can see only that he's shrugging; she can't tell his mental state.

18 SHOW ONE THING AT A TIME

We read in a linear fashion, adding words until we get the meaning of a phrase, a sentence. We can't read two parts of a sentence at the same time. Therefore, even although two events happen at the same time, they must be presented one after the other.

If you try to represent simultaneous events on the page, the reader tries to keep one thing in mind while she has to add another. There's no need for this. We want to make it as easy as possible for the reader. Instead of saying 'As she walked towards the office door, she unbuttoned her blouse', you could just as easily say 'She walked towards the office door and unbuttoned her blouse.' The simultaneous actions are presented in a linear way without detracting from the meaning. This is particularly important for longer sentences, or in complicated scenes where a lot is happening at the same time.

The linear presentation of text means also means we don't need to use 'then' very often in sequencing events. Overuse of 'then' gives a childish tone. We can accomplish sequencing by using either 'and' or a full stop and a new sentence. 'Then' is implied: 'She reached the office and unbuttoned her blouse.'

19 USE OBJECTIVITY

Objectivity relates to things that are real and factual, outside of any observer. An example objective statement might be that your character has a boss called Nigel. Subjectivity relates to what people think, believe or imagine. Subjectively, your character might say that her boss is the hottest thing on two legs.

In writing, you can distinguish between the objective and the subjective. You can show the subjective in statements that refer to your character, for example 'She ached for him.' But there is no need to involve your character in descriptions of the objective. You don't need to say: 'She could see that his office door was closed.' All you need is: 'His office door was closed.' It's the same for any other sensory input that doesn't involve interpretation – instead of 'she felt his stubble rasp against her cheek', you can say 'his stubble rasped against her cheek'. It's objective and we'll believe you.

Edit exercise

Read the latest draft of your 'Two People Meet' story.

- Can you see anything in your work that contradicts any of these principles? If there is, identify how you could change your work to meet the principles and write alternative sections.
- Do these alternatives improve your writing? If so, change them. If not, ditch them. You have the final say.

Copying and editing

There's a lot to learn from other writers' writing.

Find two pieces of erotic fiction, one that you think has been well written, and one that you think has been poorly written. Short stories from anthologies would be ideal. You might try the first chapter of novels or novellas.

- Copy these stories. Write or type them out. Include the title and the author's name.
- As you write, think about each sentence. Consider the way it has been structured and the things that the writer has included in it. Notice what the writer has done well or done badly, and mark it up on the manuscript. What can you learn from the writing? Think about each word. Is that the best word for the job?
- How does the writing in these stories compare with the principles in this chapter? Look through the chapter again and check for each point.
- Edit the stories. Make suggestions for improvement. Use a red pen if you like. Give each story a mark out of ten. If you had to pick only one principle to make the biggest improvement in each story, what would it be?
- For the purposes of this exercise only, write a better version of the stories, or of parts of them.

Focus points

This chapter presented short introductions to some of the principles of wordcraft.

- If you haven't come across these principles before, you may find that there's a lot for you to learn.
- If you haven't written much before, it's possible that you don't 'get' all of the principles. Don't worry. Your work doesn't have to be even close to perfect to reach an appreciative audience.
- Take on board what you can and make it your intention to write well. You'll be able apply more of the principles as you gain experience.
- Keep writing.

Where to next?

From principles that are relevant to all writing genres, we turn in the next chapter to issues specific to our genre. Writing isn't easy. Writing about sex has many pitfalls. We'll help you avoid them.

8

Writing about sex

How do you feel about readers masturbating when they read your work? Some of them will. They might incorporate your sex scenes into their fantasy repertoire. Some readers will use your work as a sex manual, learning from you how to introduce the kink that you've written about, even though you didn't include safe sex information because it's only supposed to be a story. Some will read the sex scenes with interest and then move on to the rest of the story because sex is just part of the bigger narrative. Some might think your sex scenes suck, and they'll tell other people that, too.

When you're writing, it can feel as though you are exposing the depths of your psyche for others to criticize. When you're writing about sex, that sense of exposure is heightened. Some find that a thrilling prospect. Many writers will want to make sure that they are not making fools of themselves. They want to write sex right.

Lily Harlem, author

'The physical mechanics, what goes where, is all very well when writing about sex (use a Barbie and a Ken doll if you need to; they don't seem to mind) but we all know that sex is about so much more than two desirous bodies coming together. To write a good sex scene, make sure your reader knows why these two (or three or four) people have tumbled into bed. Are they friends turned lovers? A married couple on a weekend away? Give your characters a history or, even better, a conflict that's made this sexy moment a struggle to reach and therefore all the more special.'

Pet hates

Loathe it, change it

The more you read erotic fiction, the easier it is to identify what you like and what you dislike in sex scenes.

- Start a list of the things you've loathed when you've read them in sex scenes.
- For each item on the list, note what you plan to do instead of that.
- Think about the language that was used, the characters, plot, setting, descriptions of sex, and the featured sex acts. You might find it helpful to reread the scenes you have in mind.
- Have at least three things on your list, ten if you can manage it. Add to it as you read more. This is your statement of intent for your sex scenes.

The things that you loathe, someone else will like. As a result, much of the erotic fiction available may not be to your taste. So thank goodness you're going to write stuff you do like, and get it out there for everyone else who likes the same things.

Here's part of our personal list:

- We hate novels that open with a sex scene. Instead, have a slow build-up and care about the character first. (It's fine when short stories and flash get into sex scenes quickly.)

- We hate sex involving two or more people who are routinely 'out there', like swingers. Instead, have characters who think 'Never in my wildest dreams would I have believed I'd do that.'
- We hate euphemisms for genitalia with adjectives attached ('throbbing manhood'). Instead, use direct language, category permitting.
- We hate having to draw diagrams to understand where all the limbs and appendages are. Instead, don't get caught up in the rush – take time to explain the spatial aspects of the scene as well as the emotional.

The things that we dislike in erotic fiction aren't created by writers who want to alienate us. It's just that we have different views about what's sexy or what works. Some of them won't have given it much thought, but they've hit on a way of writing that seems OK. Don't be that kind of writer. Make conscious creative choices. Figure out what doesn't work for you and find alternatives.

The build-up

The zoologist Desmond Morris gained international fame when he turned his scientific eye on to a rather unusual species of ape, *Homo sapiens*. Anyone who's ever seen a natural history programme will know that zoologists are interested in the way animals reproduce. In his 1971 book *Intimate Behaviour*, Morris identified 12 separate stages for the normal progression of intimacy in a couple, starting as strangers and becoming lovers:

1	Eye to body	7	Mouth to mouth
2	Eye to eye	8	Hand to head
3	Voice to voice	9	Hand to body
4	Hand to hand	10	Mouth to breast
5	Arm to shoulder	11	Hand to genitals
6	Arm to waist	12	Genitals to genitals

The stages were based upon heterosexual couples, but they can be taken as a basis for other combinations.

Stage by stage

As we go through each of Morris's stages, identify:

- the conflict that may arise, either between the couple or with a third party
- the sensory details that a point-view character will receive
- the changing emotional climate.

1 Eye to body

There's enormous satisfaction in eyeing people up and, now that you're a writer, you get to call it research. The next time you're in a busy public place, find a spot where you can admire the humanity around you. Then notice the things that you notice about people. Try to be specific; nail the precise detail. What, exactly, is attractive about them? You might like one person's build, another's clothes, and someone else's smile. Make notes so that you can remember the eye-catching details when you create characters.

You'll enjoy writing about characters you find attractive – even the baddies. When your characters are eyeing each other up, have them notice the things that you noticed.

To hone your eye for detail, can you find something attractive in everyone, even those who are not your type?

2 Eye to eye

As you people-watch, be aware of what happens when you catch someone's eye. If that other person is a stranger, you won't hold gazes for long. There are signs in a well-known London pet sanctuary that ask visitors not to stare at the dogs, as it makes them nervous. It's the same with humans – a stranger's prolonged and unbroken stare is interpreted as aggression. It's fine to gaze without inhibition at a stranger who doesn't know that you're staring at them, but you may feel embarrassed if you're caught in the act.

If you share repeated glances with a stranger, it may well be a sign of mutual sexual interest. Longer episodes of gazing into each other's eyes signify an emotional and trusting relationship.

In seconds, how long would you feel comfortable locking gazes with an attractive stranger?

3 Voice to voice

Eventually, someone starts the conversation rolling. If the point-of-view (POV) character is interested, she'll analyse what's being said and how it's being said. We can tell a lot when we hear someone speak for the first time. We get an idea, however accurate, of the kind of person they are.

Genre fiction readers love dialogue and the verbal interplay between the lead and the love interest. We skip chunks of description, even in the best books, to get to the next talking scene. Much of the joy of dialogue relates to subtext, when the reader understands what's not being said. Characters generally don't just come out and say exactly what's on their minds. You may not be able to control your thoughts or feelings, but you will usually apply a censor to the words that come out of your mouth. Because of this, body language and tone play a big part in revealing what's going on in non-POV characters' minds.

If stage 1 and 2 have been flirtatious, that tone may continue in stage 3.

Can you think of any scenario where either or both characters do not speak? What do they do instead?

4 Hand to hand

Certain types of hand-to-hand touching do not have sexual overtones in everyday life. Shaking hands or holding out a helpful hand are acts of politeness. However, put a sexy character at the other end of that arm, and hand-to-hand contact gains significance.

As voice-to-voice contact goes on, brief hand-to-arm touching may lead to longer contact, and eventually to hand-to-hand contact. As the first physical contact, it's worth describing it in detail.

If both characters are happy to hold hands, that's an undeniable sign of interest in taking things further, and the POV character will react. The characters may make the most of excuses to hold hands, for example walking to the dance floor and then while dancing.

How might characters be forced to hold hands?

5 Arm to shoulder

Morris suggests that the next small increase in intimacy is the man placing his arm around the woman's shoulder This reminds us of the drive-in scene in the film *Grease* when Danny drapes his arm around Sandy's shoulder, solely to enable him to make immediate progress to a stage that we'll call 9.5, hand to breast. Sandy is not pleased – he skipped lots of stages!

As men will put their arms around each other's shoulders in a comradely way, Morris says that this is the last step of intimacy that can be interpreted as non-sexual.

What excuses might a character make for arm-to-shoulder contact?

6 Arm to waist

Again, dancing facilitates arm-to-waist contact in a public arena. And the intimate sensation of a hand on the small of the back, ostensibly for guidance, often denotes possession.

In what other ways can you envisage arm- or hand-to-waist contact taking place between two characters?

7 Mouth to mouth

The kiss. Stage 7 is the point of no return. Until now, either party can back out with little or no loss of face, but the kiss is an absolute and unequivocal admission of sexual attraction, and it changes everything. No matter how much we've been relying on subtext until now, a kiss blatantly declares 'I fancy you'. It's confirmation of vulnerability. If you've ever been properly kissed by someone for whom you don't feel the slightest attraction, you'll appreciate that the kiss is overwhelmingly intimate.

When the kiss is accepted, it's often accompanied by a close embrace. This may be the first full body-to-body contact between the kissers, and will warrant lots of sensory description. Often, people learn to kiss during snogging sessions before they are fully sexually active. A great kiss can catapult your characters and your readers back to that adolescent time of sexual tension and longing.

But you can start small – the lightest brush of lips across lips may pack a huge sensual punch. Take your time over the first kiss. Allow the characters and the readers to revel in it. All the details, please, even if the first kiss comes after the sex.

Who was the best kisser you've known, and what was so good about it?

8 Hand to head

Hands will sneak in on the action as kisses progress in intensity. Stroking and cupping of the face is romantic, fingers running through hair is sexy, and the earlobes come into play as an erogenous zone. More sexual charge leads to pulling on hair to angle the head back, raising the mouth further. Holding the back of the head in place increases the pressure of the kiss. Angling the partner's head allows the kiss to be deepened.

What would be the effect of your characters not having full use of hands or arms at this stage, and how could you arrange this?

9 Hand to body

The characters will be keen to touch the physical features that they've admired from stage 1 onwards. It's possible that both characters will be fully dressed as this stage begins. The sensation of flesh under clothing yields sensory details relating to warmth, shape, softness, hardness, the tactile effect of fabrics, and the way clothing moves over skin. Your character will notice and think about unusual sensations first.

The characters may want to progress to skin-on-skin contact, and clothing will be removed. There's no need to go into every detail of the undressing – it's difficult to have socks removed sexily. If you describe everything but the socks coming off, the reader may well assume that he's kept his socks on – not a good look. It's worth studying how your favourite writers go about getting everyone naked, or naked enough to continue the action.

In some circumstances, clothing may not be removed, but may be opened or pulled aside to allow access for the following three stages.

At the end of this stage, which items of clothing will your characters still have on?

10 Mouth to breast

Breasts are likely to have been touched through clothes at stage 9. At stage 10, the mouth meets the breasts, perhaps first of all through underwear, and then on skin. A female partner's breasts warrant a lot of attention. Again, describe in detail what it feels like, either to give that attention or to receive it. Hands will stroke, cup and gently tug. Lips will kiss and suck, tongues lick, and teeth may tease and graze. Some women can reach orgasm through stimulation of the breasts alone – lucky, or what?

Women find men's chests interesting as a contrast to their own breasts, and enjoy touching and kissing them, too: flat, possibly muscular planes, chest hair and sensitive nipples that also like to be stimulated. At this stage, characters may have significant skin-to-skin contact for the first time. Describe the sensations. It's likely that both are fully aroused by now and showing signs of it, including erect nipples, erect penis and lubricated vagina. The rush of blood might be making them ache.

What would happen, to the characters and the reader, if the sequence was interrupted and called to a halt now?

11 Hand to genitals

Again, think about the sensations of touching and of being touched. A female character may briefly consider the shape, size and colour of the male's erect penis. Don't assume the bigger the better – your reading audience is more sophisticated and realistic than that. It's less common for the male character to pass similar comment on the female genitals, possibly primarily because the POV character for the sex scene is likely to be the female. However, the man sometimes comments on the heat and wetness of the vagina. Hand-to-genitals leads to heightened arousal as bodies prepare for penetration.

Under what circumstances would your characters touch their own genitals?

12 Genitals to genitals

Morris says that, the first time a couple has sex, they're likely to be face to face, and probably in the missionary position. There's more about writing stage 12 in the rest of this chapter.

What type of story is likely to vary the face-to-face and missionary formula for first penetration?

Using Morris's 12 stages

Write a short story in which a couple meet for the first time and progress through Morris's 12 stages.

Start the story in a public setting, such as a gig, a party, a sporting event, at work, on public transport, at the seaside, in the park – anywhere you like, as long as there are other people around who don't want to see more than they bargained for. The couple don't want to put on a show, so at what stage do they seek privacy? This will depend on the limits for the characters involved and the norms of acceptable public behaviour within their society.

Stop at the end of stage 10 – go no further than mouth to breast. Leave the story incomplete.

Aim for 3,500 words.

ALTERING THE STAGES

Morris explains that the stages mark a gradual progression towards greater intimacy over time. Both partners must become comfortable with the current stage before moving on to the next one. The building of trust and emotional bonds supports the sexual interest.

He goes on to discuss three variations to the stages:

1 Stages may be missed out. In a relationship where love has faded, or where it was never present in the first place, the early phases up to 8 or 9 may be missed entirely; sex is a duty, consent is assumed, so there's no need to dwell on stages that build emotional attachment. Jumping directly from 1 to 12 would be the pattern of rape. Prostitution may miss out stage 7 – mouth to mouth – entirely.

2 Stages may be in a different order. Think about meeting someone online. You may know a lot about their writing voice, and their way of looking at the world, but there may be little else that you can be sure of about potential mutual attraction until you meet up in person.

3 More stages may be added. Morris says that some acts are common and yet outside the standard model. These include mouth to genitals (oral sex) and mouth to body (kissing, licking and sucking other areas).

Adapting the stages

- Do you agree with Morris's stages? Are they in the correct order?

- Can you think of other patterns where stages are left out or their order is altered, or new stages are added? How would the reasons for sex that you identified in Chapter 6 affect the stages? Adapted patterns, not following all the stages, or not having them in the conventional order, can lead to exceptionally hot scenarios.

- If these are the normal stages leading towards a first sexual encounter, what changes would you make for a later encounter between the same couple? For a committed couple in a long-term relationship, what might be the effect of going back to the first stage and working through each? How might such a situation come about?

- How could the stages be adapted for solo masturbation? What would be the effect on the character of following adapted stages in order from 1 onwards?

The stages are hardwired into us. This is how we behave as sexual *Homo sapiens*. With the potential for misinterpretation in the early stages, one character may be unsure whether the attraction they feel for another is reciprocated. The other character may be focused elsewhere, with no intention of becoming sexually involved with anyone. But the reader knows how to recognize a nascent sexual relationship. Characters oh-so-subtly betray their vulnerability; subconsciously, we spot the stages, we read the signs. The reader knows more than the characters, and waits for them to catch up. If you've created a story with conflict built in, the question remaining in the reader's mind is 'How will they get to a sexual relationship in spite of everything else that's going on?' The reader wants to see them together. She'll stick around to find out what happen next.

SHORT AND LONG FORM

Erotic flash fiction is likely to focus on an aspect of one of the later stages. In Remittance Girl's story 'A Quiet Revolution' in Chapter 6, the characters are engaged in the additional mouth-to-genitals stage.

Erotic short stories may refer only in passing to the earlier stages, or may move through them quickly. They often concentrate more on events starting from stage 7, mouth to mouth.

Erotic fiction novels and novellas have space to address the whole sequence. Readers like to be teased with the slow burn of a new relationship. Indeed, it can be difficult to keep the reader interested in the sex once the characters have fully committed to each other. More of the same isn't of great interest. So the writer may add unconventional sexual practices to keep the reader's interest.

Morris, however, suggests that the normal sequence is enough for couples who are in love and newly sexually involved, and that the variations from the sexual norm are only necessary once the first flush wears off. Do you agree with this? A popular way of avoiding reader boredom is by establishing early on that one character has unconventional sexual interests, and have them slowly initiate their partner into their erotic world.

LESS THAN PERFECT SEX

Sometimes, a story will call for things to go wrong between the sheets. This might be because your lead and love interest haven't found each other yet; they're involved with other partners, and the sex is OK, but not mind blowing. Perhaps the conflict inherent in their sexual contact means that your characters don't get fully into the liaison. Maybe an external conflict interrupts the proceedings and they're left wanting more.

Think about Morris's stages in relation to every sexual experience in your story. Adapt stages or skip them to create the groundwork for less-than-perfect sex.

The main act

As a member of the human race, you know Morris's stages already. You've lived by them, Morris catalogued them, and now we've raised them to the conscious part of your mind. As a writer, the stages can be a map, showing you the major landmarks as your characters carry on towards their sexual destination.

Readers know how sex works. Sex scenes are sometimes written as an objective description, as though they are porn videos described on the page. Only the external aspects are narrated – who does what to whom, what bits go where. Erotic fiction readers do need to understand what is going on externally, but much of the power of sex scenes lies in the subjective, in the feeling and thoughts of the POV character and in the reader's empathy with that character. Good sex scenes must get the both the external acts and the internal reactions right.

You know how sex works, too. This isn't a sex manual and we couldn't hope to do justice to the variety of sexual expression. But sex manuals are widely available and they are an excellent source of information and ideas for writers of erotic fiction. They come in a range of tones from verging on the clinical, to mystical, to good fun for all. You should be able to find at least one that suits you.

 Remittance Girl, author

'*Erotica is not really about sex; it's about how sex and sexual desire affect us, change us, evolve us. The actual details of the sex are only important because of the semiotic meaning we, as a culture, adorn it with. From a mechanistic perspective, there is little difference between vaginal and anal penetration, but to the person experiencing the act, the difference is tremendous. How it feels, what it says about us and the person we do it with are the reasons these acts have enduring significance for us and reverberate into our subjective understanding of who we are and how we orient ourselves to the world.*'

We are interested in helping you to structure your sex scenes. Here are some points to remember:

- Erotic fiction relates to consensual sex between adults.
- Sex between the lead character and the love interest is usually a positive experience. Sometimes, things may start out on a negative note and end positive (when the sex takes place because of conflict) and sometimes sex may start positive and become negative (when the sex leads to conflict). Generally, though, the participants are having a good time.
- Sex in erotic fiction usually leads to at least one orgasm for each participant.
- The sex has meaning in the context of your story – it's not gratuitous.

PLANNING THE SEX SCENE

To be certain that your sex scenes are not gratuitous, think about how they fit into the story as a whole. Remember that the sex is never just about the sex. It's about characters that we've come to know and like, placing themselves in positions of intimacy.

- How will this sex scene change things in the story? Will something be revealed? Will someone act in a way that has repercussions?
- How will this sex scene affect your lead, your love interest, or anyone else involved? How will you show that they have been affected?

When you're happy that the sex has purpose in the story, plan the steps within the sex scene, just as you would for any other scene.

- Where and when does the scene take place? What happened to the characters involved immediately before the scene started?
- What is the POV character's goal – what does she want? Remember that this should be concrete; you should be able to take a photograph of her achieving it.
- What's a stake?
- How do obstacles arise, creating conflict?
- How does she react?
- Does she fail to achieve her goal, or does she succeed?
- How will you leave the reader wondering about what happens next?

WRITING THE SEX SCENE

Tabitha Rayne, author

'I think that if you are writing erotica to elicit a physical or emotional response from your reader, then, as a writer, it has to do the same to you. If you are still feeling turned on and excited by your work after 8 drafts and 13 rounds of editing – then you can be a little more confident that your reader will be, too! There has to be a point where you cast aside any self-consciousness to enable you to do this. You have to be confident enough to use the language that excites you.'

A lot of erotic fiction is about 'vanilla' sex. Just as vanilla ice cream is common and unremarkable without any added extras, vanilla sex refers to conventional sex between a heterosexual couple, without any kinky variations. It will involve some foreplay as preparation for penetrative sex. There are similar versions of vanilla for gay and for lesbian sex. As a beginning writer, we'd advise you to start with vanilla and build up from there.

Here are some tips for writing convincingly about sex:

- **Involve all of the senses.** And if one sense is removed, for example the lead can't see because it's pitch dark, her other senses are heightened and it adds tension. What is the love interest going to do next?

- **Don't fixate on describing the genitals, or how the sex act looks.** Sure it's of interest, but you don't need too much of this.

- **Make sure you stay in the head of the POV character** – you can't get the other character's thoughts or intentions. The only indication of their mental state is what they say or do.

- **Follow objective with subjective.** Every time you write about an objective event, something an observer could see happening, follow it up with a separate sentence (or more) about what the POV character feels or thinks about that event. For example, when the love interest peels off the lead's knickers, what does the lead think? What does she do or say? The lead's action or speech is the next objective event. Then what does she think or feel about her own reaction? How does her lover react to what's she's said? Keep up this pattern of action and reaction, bouncing back and forward between the two characters. Tell us enough about the action so that we understand what's going on, but concentrate more on what it feels like to be involved in that act.

- **Make the most of dialogue.** Good sex relies on good communication, both non-verbal and verbal. At the early stages, don't settle for 'Oh my God!' and 'Wow!' Have your characters talk to each other, flirtatiously, or teasingly, or competitively, or romantically, or whatever works best, according to their personalities. This will show more about their character and the nature of their relationship. As they get close to orgasm, your characters will say less, speaking in fragments of sentences, or single words. Eventually, they might not be able to use proper words at all. It's better to use indirect speech, such as 'He groaned' than it is to report direct incoherent speech such as 'Graargh!'

- **Show the reader any changes in the POV character's emotional state.** Her emotions will depend upon many things, including the reason for having sex. If it is sex due to conflict, her emotions at the start and at the end of the encounter may be very different from sex that causes conflict.

- **Ensure that both characters reach orgasm at least once, and in a credible way.** The English translation of the Japanese term for male masturbation is 'a hundred rubs'. For female masturbation, it's 'ten thousand rubs'. That says it all. From anecdotal evidence, we believe that most women don't have vaginal orgasms during their first sexual intercourse. Just saying.

- When you've finished a first draft, go back and **take out all the describing words:** the adverbs and adjectives. These are usually superfluous. Where you've removed an adverb, try other verbs until you get exactly the right word for the action. You may decide to put some of the adjectives back in, but restrict yourself to using only those that are necessary to convey information to your reader. For example, you don't need to tell us about his 'rigid shaft'. If he's doing *that* with it, we already get that it's rigid.

Despite everything that we've said here, if you've got a good reason for doing the opposite, go ahead. Whatever works, works.

Finishing Morris's 12 stages

Now look at the story you started, based on Morris's 12 stages. It's time to pick it up from where you left off.

- Read over what you've already written and assess your work in relation to the questions in the 'Planning the sex scene' section above. Rewrite as necessary.

- Complete the sexual contact by writing stages 11 and 12, hand to genitals and genitals to genitals. At this stage, don't worry about using the 'right' words. Just let the story flow from you. Intend to write a vanilla scene, but if you find yourself straying into something less conventional, go with it.

- Write on until the end of the story. Does the lead achieve her goal? What has changed for her?

- Aim for 1,500 words for this section of the story. You should end up with 5,000 words in total.
- Once you're happy with this story, put it aside. Don't lose it.

VARIETY

 Hazel Cushion, CEO Xcite Books

'People are very into spanking—it's the new black.'

There are many things that can be varied from the standard vanilla model, whether that is heterosexual or homosexual vanilla. Here are a few.

1 Oral

From scalp to toes and everything in between, there are many ways to touch and stimulate sensitive parts of the body. Be inventive. Let your characters explore each other. Where do you love to lick or be licked? While much of this isn't necessarily outside the vanilla experience, some parts of the body are less conventional erotic zones than others and we enter the realms of kink. For example, oculolinctus refers to arousal from licking the partner's eyeballs.

2 Positions

Vary sexual positions. For penetrative sex, you can vary which partner is on top, with rear entry a possibility either way. Or put neither on top, having them lying side by side, sitting or standing. Just be sure that what you are writing about is physically possible. For non-penetrative positions, there's an expanded set of options because genitals don't need to be in close proximity to each other.

3 Props

Props can be introduced into the sex scene. Clothing, bedding and other furniture can all be put to use. Light BDSM play can involve household objects, with fun being found in a hairbrush or a shower head. Sex toys are another alternative. If your characters use props, make sure that there's a good reason for the prop being to hand, or show them going to fetch it. Most people don't keep cucumbers under their pillows.

4 Location

Take the sex out of the bedroom. Think of other places in the home in the first instance, or semi-private places such as the lead's office at work. Then they can go public. If there's a danger of getting caught, there are additional sexual thrills for the lovers and more tension for the reader.

5 Performance and voyeurism

Either in a public place or facilitated by modern technology, the urge to show off and to observe can add spice to sexual encounters.

6 BDSM

Expanded to the full, BDSM stands for 'bondage and discipline, domination and submission, and sadism and masochism'. There's been a glut of BDSM novels recently, and this seems to be a popular if crowded sub-genre. The most successful stories involve a young, somewhat naive woman and an older, sexually dominant man. Dominant women do not have the same appeal in the commercial market (yet). BDSM often involves the dominant partner restricting movement and administering controlled amounts of pain to the submissive partner. Therefore, it is an area that must be fully researched before you write about it, to ensure that you are not passing on unsafe practice, and to make sure that you retain credibility.

7 Anal

Anal sex and anal play is another area where care must be exercised by the writer to ensure that readers don't compromise their own health by copying risky practice. If you don't do this already, research it properly if you intend to write about it.

8 Gay (or straight) for you

Stories may involve a character who normally identifies as heterosexual becoming involved with someone of the same sex, as a result of attraction to that specific person. Similarly, normally homosexual characters may become sexually interested in someone of the opposite sex. That's a powerful message – you're so attractive that it overrides my normal sexual orientation. Although that's probably not the most romantic way to say it.

9 Multiple partners

The addition of a third person to a stable couple is known as a *ménage à trois*. Three individuals coming together for sex is a threesome, four is a foursome, sometimes made up of two couples. Any more than four and we're into orgy territory. If it's four men and one woman, you've got a gang bang, and four women and one man is a reverse gang bang. There are a couple of problems with multiple-partner scenarios. First of all, the more people you add into a sex scene, the harder it is to keep track of all of the limbs and appendages – make sure you've got the right number of bits in the scene at any one time. Secondly, the requirement of erotic fiction is the emotional element of the sexual relationship. As you add more bodies, it gets progressively more difficult for the reader to believe in an emotional connection.

10 Kink

BDSM practices can be regarded as a subset of kink. Kink is a general name for unconventional sexual activities. For those who are not sexually aroused by the same acts or substances, kink can be amusing, difficult to understand, or even regarded as obscene. That's a great source of conflict. Examples of kink might be arousal caused by animal fur or skin, or the use of insects during sex play, or scat (faeces). Many aspects of kink are too niche for conventional publishers and the wider reading public. Writers may struggle to find anything more than a niche audience for stories about highly specialized desires.

 Beyond vanilla

Which of the non-vanilla sexual flavours have you tasted? Do you fantasize about something you haven't tried? These would be appropriate subjects for future stories.

Can you come up with a story idea for each of the ten non-vanilla scenes listed above? If the writing's good enough, it's possible to be turned on when we read about sexual practices that we don't particularly want to experience, that wouldn't normally do it for us. When you're a more experienced writer, see if you can create a convincing story about a practice that leaves you cold. The creative process may help you find enough sexiness in the act to give the story credibility, and you'll have learned a bit more about both yourself and other people.

Putting it into words

There are lots of different sexual words available. You need to choose the right ones. If you get it wrong, you'll trip up the reader. During the sex scenes, more than at any other time, the reader needs to feel that she can trust the writer. She doesn't want the words to get in the way of the flow of images. The sex scene is a crucial part of the developing relationship (isn't it?), she's looked forward to it, and she wants you to get it right.

You'll know what you like and what you don't like from your own reading. There are three guidelines to help you choose the right words – the heat, the character and the craft.

HEAT WORDS

In Chapter 1, we discussed the various sub-genres in erotic fiction and the heat levels. Certain publishing imprints may accept only particular heat levels, and the vocabulary associated with those levels. Therefore, it is again essential for you to get to know the sub-genre that you are writing for. Read widely. Identify the words that can be used generally and the risky ones that you might get away with once in a while. Be prepared to edit the risky ones out of your work if requested.

You'll need words to cover all bases. What words do you use in real life? It's possible that you'll use different words when you're talking to a partner over dinner from those you'd use during sex, or if you're talking to your best friend, or your mother, or your doctor. Perhaps there are some words that you would never use, but you don't mind reading them. Others may be completely taboo as far as you are concerned.

In each of the following examples, we've gone from least to most heat.

- **Intercourse** – make love or have sex or fuck?
- **Male sexual characteristics** – manhood or penis or prick or cock? Throbbing member (no!) or erection? Testicles or balls? As a verb, ejaculate or orgasm or come or cum? As a noun, ejaculate or semen or spunk or cum?
- **Female sexual characteristics** – core or vagina or pussy or cunt? Pearl or button or clitoris or clit? Bosom or breasts or tits? Moisture or wetness or juices?

Another option is the 'say nothing' approach. In this case, you might say 'he entered her' or 'he held himself' or 'she touched herself'. Although this comes across as a bit coy, the reader will be able to follow what's not being said. This option is most often found at the cooler end of the spectrum. At the hotter end, it's an option that may be used alongside more explicit terms.

You do have a bit of scope to go up and down the heat scale, but let other work in your target market help you define the absolute limits.

CHARACTERS' WORDS

The scope to move up and down the heat scale helps you to accommodate another variable. Just as you change your vocabulary to suit your situation, your characters will use specific words in their speech according to the context. Your POV character will use particular words in her thoughts, and therefore these are the words used in the filter that you apply to a scene. Her choice of vocabulary also needs to be situation appropriate, heat appropriate and character appropriate. That's a lot to juggle.

Characters' words might be more idiosyncratic or jocular than normal if your writing admits a bit of comedy. If you don't play any of it for laughs, however, it's best to keep Mr Wang and the Fuzzy Froo-froo out of it.

Characters' interests may provide good opportunities for descriptive writing about the sensations of sex. For example, a skier may think about sex in terms of the rush and the adrenalin and the towering majesty of the mountains, and a cool whiteout at orgasm. Luckily, no one knows exactly what's in another person's mind as they climax. Use this to your advantage, and write with authority.

CRAFT

Writing erotic fiction is still writing, and there's still scope for some beautifully crafted descriptions of the sensations linked to sex. As long as they're not forced or overblown, there's room for the perfect simile or metaphor in sex scenes.

Avoid similes or metaphors that you've heard before – they are often clichés. As you read, look out for orgasms that are compared with natural disasters. Earthquakes, eruptions, tidal waves, tornados, infernos … we've seen 'em all, many times.

If you find a cliché in your own writing, think about what you were trying to do. Explain it in your own words. You may find that, without the cliché to hide behind, you come up with a more honest account of what sex fees like.

Erotic fiction isn't eligible for the annual Bad Sex in Fiction Award run by the *Literary Review*. That's a relief. However, we can learn from the mistakes made by the shortlist and winners. The worst passages often rely on scientific terms, or they are terribly gauche, or they include distinctly unsexy comparisons that refer to the action of sex rather than the sensation of it. Check out past winners of the award and work out for yourself where they went wrong.

Do notice and take note when writers of any genre use their craft well to describe the experience of sex and orgasm. Despite the over-reliance on natural disasters, other aspects of the natural world seem to lend themselves comfortably to descriptive writing. Images concerning light, water, weather and natural environments often work well.

Lucy Felthouse, author

'Remember not to use words that will make people laugh (unless you're writing comedy, obviously), like comparing male genitalia to root vegetables, or female to flowers. Keep it simple, and bear in mind that there are only so many words you can use, so you may well have to use ones you don't like to avoid repetition. Work hard at these scenes in the beginning, and you'll find it much easier as you continue writing. Make it realistic, sexy and passionate. If it makes you hot, it's working.'

Focus points

Sex is, at the same time, both intensely private and ubiquitous. People like to think about it, do it and talk about it. Many readers miss it when stories stop at the bedroom door. They want your characters to engage in successful intimate relationships. As a minimum, they want to be entertained by your story and, at best, they want to be turned on.

If you want to get it right, mastering erotic fiction requires as much skill and hard work as other genres, and some more hard work again because sex can easily strike the wrong note on the page. We respect anyone who has the guts to try.

Things to remember

- If you don't like what you see in erotic fiction, you can change it in your own work.
- The shorter the story, the fewer of Morris's stages are required.
- Readers know how sex works – you don't need to describe every thrust.
- There's really no need for gratuitous sex.
- Vanilla is the most popular flavour. People like it.
- Some of them like everything else, too. Go beyond vanilla when your comfort zone and your research knowledge are ready.

Things to do

- Even unaware readers know Morris's stages intimately. Use them as a structure but play around with them, too.
- Plan a sex scene just as you would any other. They are significant events and need careful handling as far as storytelling and wordcraft are concerned.
- Know the words your character uses and your category expects.
- Describe the sensations and experience of sex, not just the mechanics or the visuals.
- Banish clichés – think about what you're trying to say, and say it in your own way.

Where to next?

The next chapter rounds off our discussion of skills relating to writing well. You've gathered inspiration and set out your vision over the course of the first eight chapters, and you've written a few stories, too. Before you send those stories off into the wide world, you'll want to be certain that they're as good as you can make them at the moment. No one stands to gain if you send work out before it's ready. We'll help you polish those erotic gems in Chapter 9 – Revision.

9

Revision

Ernest Hemingway declared that 'the first draft of anything is shit'. Experienced writers know this, and they write more than one draft of their stories. Revision, redrafting, editing: whatever we call it, we must ensure that the best possible version of our work is out there. Don't waste readers' time and goodwill by circulating the shit.

As with planning, some people love revision, and some people hate it. It still needs to be done. In this short chapter, we'll take you through an efficient method of revising your work; you can be confident that time allocated to this part of the writing process will be time well spent.

The system of revision in this chapter covers all the key elements of writing. Give it a go. After trying it, you might decide that you want to break the levels down further, building in more drafts. Or you may want to roll them together, revising everything at the same time in one big chunk. Whatever you decide, use the elements as a checklist, and adapt the levels to suit your preferred way of working.

If you've been following the exercises in this book, you have drafts of at least five separate stories:

- From Chapter 2, a 500-word story about 'The First Time'
- From Chapter 3, a 1,000-word story based on a memory
- From Chapter 4, a 1,600-word story about two people meeting and having sex, revised in Chapter 7
- From Chapter 6, a 3,000-word story based on an outline
- From Chapter 8, a 5,000-word story based on Morris's 12 stages of intimacy.

This will give you plenty to revise. Have these stories to hand as you progress through this chapter. If you haven't completed these exercises, either go back now and write them, or look at other work you've written, or pick other writers' short stories of varying lengths from a collection or anthology and work on these for now.

We carried out some small-scale revision in Chapters 7 and 8. Now, we're going to expand that process, make it more structured, and give you logical steps to follow.

Why revise?

Nothing should come in the way of the flow of images that your story delivers to readers' minds. If the flow is stopped, the reader is bumped out of your story. Bump her out too often and she might remember all those other demands on her time, the things she should be doing instead of reading, or the other enticing stories that she hasn't read yet. The flow stops when she can't follow what's going on, when story events are implausible, when characters are inconsistent, when things don't ring true, when the writing is too complicated or too patronizing, and when we make mistakes. When we revise, we're getting rid of the things that interrupt the flow.

If you are writing only for yourself – as often happens in the early stages of a writing career – you can get away with not revising your work. This will certainly save you time, time that you can use to write another story. But this would be a false economy. As a writer, you will learn from your own mistakes. Once you've gone through a 100,000-word novel, taking out all the adverbs and strengthening the verbs, you're less likely to rely on adverbs the next time you write a first draft. Critiquing your own work, when you know what to look for, is a learning experience. It'll make you a better writer in a shorter time.

When to start

Most writers revise a little as they go along, changing words and altering sentences as they are being written. Some writers start the day by reading and tweaking their text from the day before. This is a good way of finding your place in the story again. However, when revision stops you from writing the next section, it becomes a problem.

You should have an idea by now of how many words you write in a day. We suggested in Chapter 2 that everyone could find 15 minutes daily, and that 225 words would be a reasonable target for those 15 minutes. Hopefully, you've written at least five pieces since then, and you'll have found that 225 words is fine for a daily minimum, but you're happy to write more than that on a good day. So, what are you aiming for? Five hundred words a day? A thousand?

Whatever your target, make sure that you hit it with new writing, not rewriting pages that you did earlier. Move your story on. Yes, the section you did yesterday might need some more work, but you don't need to do that work now. It's more important that you finish your first draft. Why? Because lots of stories get started and don't get finished, because you can't get an overview of your story until it's complete, and because you can't find an audience until it's a full story. (Some websites carry the latest instalments of works-in-progress. However, you still need to have completed scenes or chapters ready to post.)

We recommend taking the following steps:

- You finish a full first draft before undertaking a major revision of your work. If you need to change some details in an earlier section, write a note to yourself as a reminder or annotate the manuscript, but keep moving forward.
- You wait until you have some distance from a piece before you revise it, until you've partially forgotten what you have written. Come to it fresh. This helps you see what you've put on the page rather that what was in your mind as you wrote.

- You can get distance by waiting for some time to pass before you look at your work again. One month is a good rule of thumb; more is better if you can manage it. This waiting time can be dramatically shortened if you are doing lots of writing in the intervening period. If you're working to a deadline, remember to build distancing and revision time into your writing schedule. Whatever you do, don't send in your first draft. Remember Hemingway.

When to stop

In our experience, the best way to stop revising is hitting a deadline. You have to pass your story on to someone else. Otherwise, it's possible to carry on indefinitely, tweaking here and there, adding bits and taking others away.

Competitions and calls for submission are good sources of deadlines. Or you may decide that the story must be finished before a particular event in your life. Many people promise themselves that they're going to write a novel in the year before, or after, a big birthday or another major milestone.

Aside from deadlines, how do you know when you've finished revising? You may just have a feeling that the story is ripe. It's said that you need to stop when your changes are making the story worse, not better. But one way to know for certain that you're done is to follow a structured programme of revision – stop when you get to the end of the process. That's what we're covering in the next section.

How to revise

We are going to revise your story on three separate levels, in the following order:

1 the structural level
2 the scene level
3 the sentence level.

At each level, we will give you a checklist that prompts you to consider different aspects of your story. At the end of level 3, your revision will be complete.

We revise in this order because there's no point in messing about with level 3 details such as word choice or punctuation when the sentence is part of a level 2 scene that has to be deleted because it doesn't fit your overall level 1 structure. That would be a complete waste of time. You'd be tempted to hang on to sections that don't work, because you've put so much effort into them.

Revision often entails a lot of cutting, and that can be difficult. Here are some words of encouragement:

- **Good writing is never wasted.** For one thing, you've practised writing well. For another, if you cut a good section from your current story, keep it with other cut sections in a separate file – it might be right for a later piece.

- **First ideas aren't always the best ideas.** Sometimes it's the third idea or the eighth idea that's the best one. If you suspect that your current idea for a story, or a scene, or a verb isn't good enough, you're probably right. Don't settle for the easiest, obvious options.

- **You won't run out of story ideas.** It might feel as though your current idea is the only one you'll ever have, but that's not true. Writers have more ideas than they can sensibly cram into one story, and more story ideas than they can write in a lifetime. If you're worried about this, don't despair. It's just that you haven't found the knack of capturing ideas, yet. Remember the Big Sexy List? Go back to that, and add to it. Along with your list of reasons for having sex, it's your erotic fiction ideas bank.

- **Keep a 'before' version.** If you have the security of an untouched first draft in a safe place, you'll be happier to make cuts.

What are you revising?

This section gives you revision guidelines that are suitable for novels and points out differences for other forms. If you are revising work from the exercises in this book, look at each story separately through all three levels. You will become increasingly familiar with the levels' contents. As well as making revision quicker, this will improve the first drafts of your future stories, too. Don't worry if your earlier stories, such as 'The First Time', do not meet the conventions of erotic fiction.

There are a few advantages in revising other people's work for the purposes of learning how it should and shouldn't be done. There is an inexhaustible supply of stories that could be improved. You will have the distance needed; the story will not be precious to you, and you won't know what was in the writer's mind at the time. The disadvantage is that it will take longer to work through the levels if you are less familiar with the work.

There's a lot to learn from revising your own work and someone else's. Do both if you can.

LEVEL 1: THE STRUCTURAL LEVEL

From your manuscript, create a 'map' of your story.

- If it's a novella or novel, make a list of every scene, describing in a couple of sentences what happens in each scene and where it takes place. If the point of view passes to different characters, note who the point-of-view (POV) character is for each scene. This scene list will be similar to the scene plan that you created in Chapter 6, but it probably won't be identical, as the plan often changes once you start writing.
- If it's a short story, list the main story events.

Assess your story from the map.

- Does it have a clear beginning, middle and end? Can you identify the transitions between them?
- Is there rising tension throughout the story? The toughest challenges should come at the climax scene.
- For flash fiction, does it focus on a moment of revelation in one of Morris's later stages?
- For short stories, have you included enough information from Morris's early stages to engage the reader in the relationship?
- For novels, are the seven (or eight) key scenes present and in the correct place? (Short stories can also follow this structure, possibly with sections rather than full scenes.)
  1. Opening scene
  2. Inciting Incident (as near the start as makes sense)
  3. End of Act I (one-quarter of the way through)
  4. Midpoint (halfway through)
  5. End of Act II (three-quarters through)

6 Decision point – not necessarily a separate scene

7 Climax

8 End of Act III – Wrap-up

- Is your story erotic fiction, rather than romance, or porn, or something else entirely? Sometimes, stories don't turn out as we intended. This is not a problem. You can either rewrite the story as erotic fiction, or you can leave it as it is and do some research to make sure the story meets another genre's requirements. In erotic fiction, the key scenes will be sexual.
- Does each sex scene affect the characters and plot, changing things? In other words, are they all necessary?
- Do you have the correct amount of sexual content for the category?
- If you have more than one sex scene, do you show progression and variety?
- Is there enough drama? For novels, do big events impact on characters' lives? For shorter fiction, is the level of drama appropriate?
- Are the scenes or steps in the linking sections between the seven key scenes logical? Are they less dramatic than the key scenes?
- Is every scene in the best position?
- Does each scene contribute to the overall story?
- Have you used as few settings as possible?
- Have you used as few characters as possible? Double up secondary and minor character roles.
- If you have different viewpoint characters, do they have the correct balance of viewpoint scenes, with the lead having by far the most? Count them to be certain. Are each character's viewpoint scenes distributed evenly throughout the story?
- If there's something complicated that affects any of the key scenes, have you explained this or shown an example of it in an earlier part of the story, rather than holding up an important scene while you explain?
- Does your lead character know something at the end that she didn't know at the beginning? Can you trace the change in the lead through the course of the story? Is the change believable in relation to the story events she has experienced?
- Is your ending appropriate to the sub-genre?

You should be able to answer yes to all these questions. Don't move on to the next level of revising until you can.

You may need to change the order of scenes, cut some scenes or write new scenes to fill gaps. Take as long as you need to accomplish all of this. When you have finished making changes, do a new map of your story – scene list or summary of events – and run through the structural level checks again. When you are confident that your structure is right, print out your full manuscript.

LEVEL 2: THE SCENE LEVEL

From your manuscript, skim through each scene, one scene at a time.

Assess the scene, checking that the following items are in place, and marking them on the manuscript. Mark them so that you don't just slide over the page, thinking 'Yeah, it's all there ...' We know the avoidance techniques. Marking them on your manuscript reassures you that the scene has the right ingredients.

- Check that you have included:
  1 an orientation to the place, time and POV character at the start of the scene
  2 your POV character pursuing a goal
  3 conflict – something blocks your character's attempts to achieve her goal
  4 your character taking action – physical action, dialogue or thought – that moves the story on
  5 description that is distributed throughout the scene rather than appearing in unbroken chunks
  6 a realistic representation of the passage of time, flowing in one direction, with a second-by-second account of what's going on
  7 a change in the POV character's situation or attitude by the end of the scene
  8 upbeat sex scenes, despite all the conflict
  9 things happening after the inciting incident because of character actions, not coincidence.
- If you are not following the three-act structure, make sure the story grows and builds in a way that makes sense to you. If you are following the three-act structure, assess specific scenes and linking sections, checking that they have the following:

1 Opening scene – a hook in the first paragraph to draw the reader into the story

2 Linking section 1 – introductions to the lead, love interest(s) and antagonist(s), if present (however, don't overload the reader with too many named characters appearing right at the start of the story)

3 Inciting incident – a change in the lead's life that requires action

4 Linking section 2 – the lead finds out that she cannot sort things out easily

5 End of Act I – a major change in the story (the lead becomes aware of how much she doesn't know)

6 Linking section 3 – the lead learning about her new situation, and introductions to all remaining characters by the end of the section

7 Midpoint – another change in the storyline (the lead may have an incomplete victory over the antagonist; she has learned something about her new situation)

8 Linking section 4 – the lead knows what she has to do, and faces more obstacles

9 End of Act II – another change makes the lead feels hopeless and far from achieving her goals

10 Linking section 5 – the lead coming up with a new course of action and pursuing it

11 Decision point – the lead facing a dilemma and deciding how to act

12 Climax – the final showdown (irrevocable change is made in the lead's life and attitude)

13 End of Act III, Wrap-up – the tying-up of all loose ends (we see the lasting effect of the change in the lead's life)

- For novels and novellas, you can now break your story into chapters. You may break the chapters at the point immediately before or immediately after a major revelation or change, to encourage the reader to keep reading. This may or may not be at the end of a scene. Check how your favourite writer handles chapter breaks. Chapters are usually of a similar length. Often, chapters contain three or so scenes, but a long key scene may require a chapter of its own.

Again, take as long as you need to check all these elements. If you've made any changes to a scene, rewrite it as necessary, then go back and check its structure again.

Once you're happy with your scenes, print a fresh version of your manuscript.

LEVEL 3: THE SENTENCE LEVEL

Read each scene several times before you move on to the next scene.

1 Read each sentence of the scene aloud, word for word

Yes, you may feel a bit silly, but this is the best way to spot problems; we might miss mistakes on the page but they stand out when read aloud. Does anything sound wrong, or bump you out of the story? Don't stop to change your work at this stage. Just mark the place where you stumbled and move on.

2 Read each sentence again for wordcraft issues

Look for and mark up the following problems. Go back to Chapter 7 if you need help remembering what some of them mean.

GENERAL WORDCRAFT PROBLEMS

- Amateur use of typography – bold, underlined, italics used for emphasis, too many ellipses, dashes or exclamation marks
- Complicated sentence structure
- Poor punctuation that makes sentences difficult to follow, or lets them run on too long
- Big chunks of text in single paragraphs, which are tiring to read
- An annoying tone – for example, trying too hard to be clever, or posh, or sexy
- Any dialogue tags other than 'said' or 'asked'
- Dialogue punctuation and paragraphing that don't follow the conventions, making it difficult to ascertain who is speaking
- Passive voice used when active would be better, and vice versa
- Monotonous sentence structure and length
- Telling when you should be showing the interesting stuff, particularly emotions and sex

- Showing boring or inconsequential events second by second – for example, characters drinking wine or making tea (either 'tell' them or cut them completely)
- Actions, thoughts and dialogue that bear no relation to what's going on, instead of being a reaction to something that's happened immediately before

CHARACTER-RELATED PROBLEMS
- Point of view bouncing around in different characters' heads instead of one person's for, at least, a whole scene or half of a long key scene
- The POV character thinking, speaking or acting in a way that is inconsistent with her personality
- Dialogue where characters say exactly what they are thinking
- Minor characters getting more page time than their roles warrant
- Melodramatic reactions, with characters' emotions out of proportion to events

MISSED OPPORTUNITIES
- Vague nouns
- Adverbs that show you've chosen the wrong verb
- Unvarying distance from the action
- Squandered power positions at the ends of sentences, paragraphs, scenes and chapters

FINER POINTS
- Writing about what doesn't happen, rather than what does
- Trying too hard to show lots of things happening at once
- Putting the character in objective statements

3 Rewrite the scene to get rid of the issues you've found in steps 1 and 2

Changing a sentence may mean you have to rewrite those around it.

4 Print a clean version of the scene

5 Read it aloud again

If it's fine, you've finished revising that scene – move on to the next one. If you still find parts difficult to read, or you uncover new bumps, address them before you move to the next scene. Go through these steps as many times as you need to, reading aloud every time you have a fresh manuscript in front of you.

It may take you as long to produce a good second draft as it took you to produce a first draft, or even longer. Give revision as much time as it needs.

Writing can be messy. You may start to revise a scene, or even a whole story, and think that you'd be better off starting from scratch than trying to improve your existing draft. You may be right. Sometimes, the first draft functions as thinking on the page. Don't be afraid to start again now that you have the story straight in your mind.

Outside help

For writers new to their craft, outside help can speed up the learning process.

BOOKS

There are innumerable books dedicated to every aspect of writing. In the Appendix we've recommended the ones that we've found most useful through the years. If you identify a problem with your craft during revision and we've not been able to cover it here, there's bound to be another book that can help you fix it.

If you're a committed thinker or planner, it's possible to get lost in these books. There's always something that you don't know, someone who might explain it better. Your search for the key to the mystery of writing can go on for ever. Take care. Remember that you're reading at this stage to inform your revision, not for general interest.

BUDDIES

Writing is generally a solitary pursuit. Writing circles are small groups of writers who come together every so often to offer friendship and mutual support. They often read and critique each other's work. When they work well, writing circles are motivating. These are people who understand the bittersweet experience of writing, people who might have some ideas about how to solve your creative problems or who will offer encouragement if they don't, people who will set deadlines for you.

Writing circles go wrong when they turn into an opportunity to chat rather than to focus on the writing, when they become so friendly that no one's willing to comment honestly on poor work, when they're so large that opportunities to circulate your work are few and far between, or when they are so relaxed that no one minds if you don't produce any work.

In Chapter 11 we talk about ways of finding writing friends and critique partners online.

PROFESSIONALS

Writing classes and courses are ubiquitous, from absolute beginner level to experienced writers, from informal adult education leisure courses to university postgraduate degrees, delivered face to face or online. They often combine taught elements of craft, exercises to practise those elements, and feedback from teachers and fellow students on circulated work. As well as a way to learn writing skills quickly, they can be a good place to meet like-minded writing buddies.

As you become more secure in your craft, there will come a time when taught classes are a distraction rather than a help. When you reach this stage, bow out gracefully and follow your own agenda at your own pace.

Editorial and manuscript advisory services charge fees to provide feedback on your work. Some are scouts for literary agents. We talk about professional editing services in Chapter 11.

CIRCULATING WORK AND RECEIVING CRITICISM

Circulating your work-in-progress is a risky business. Some writers are encouraged by the comments they receive; some are completely disheartened. Some circles and classes have a positive vibe; some don't. You might find that members of a general circle or class are uncomfortable critiquing your erotic fiction. Not everyone wants to go there.

On balance, it's better to circulate your work and learn what fellow writers think are your strengths and weaknesses early in your writing career. And it's good to learn how to take criticism. You don't want to be completely devastated by editors' requests for rewrites.

Listen to criticism with an open mind. The person commenting may not understand exactly what's gone wrong in your text or how to fix it but, if they've been bumped out of your story for any reason, you need to know where that happened. You might disagree with their critique. Receive their comments graciously and decide later how to act on them, if at all. The final decision is yours.

When you have more writing experience, try to avoid circulating work until you have completed both a full first draft and a revised second draft. You'll have pinned down your story at this stage, so it is less likely to be derailed by conflicting opinions. Any remaining bumps will be problems that you have missed in revision – you'll learn about your own blind spots, and you'll be mindful of them moving forward.

However experienced you are, it's good manners to revise your work as much as you can before you circulate it for external comment.

Focus points

It's said that 'writing is rewriting'. We let ourselves make a creative mess during the first draft because we know that the story will fulfil its potential when it has been revised into shape.

If you ever read a first draft of your own writing and think that it stinks, remember Hemingway. Get out your red pen, roll up your sleeves, and rewrite until you end up with a story that your readers will love.

Things to remember

- Don't expect too much from your first draft.
- You will learn from revising both your own work and someone else's.
- Revision may take longer than you thought.
- Outside help is available from books, buddies and professionals.

Things to do

- Start revising when you have a full first draft and some time has passed.
- If you don't have a deadline, stop revising when changes are making the story worse.
- Revise in order from the structural level, to the scene level, to the sentence level.
- For scene and sentence, read your work aloud.
- Receive criticism graciously but make the final decision.

Where to next?

This is the end of our tour through the three skill sets used in writing – creativity, storytelling and wordcraft. If you've been completing the exercises, you should now have five short stories.

Next, we turn to the business side of erotic fiction. This crucial fourth set of skills comes into play when you have a finished product. The following three chapters will identify ways of getting your stories into readers' hands. First off, Chapter 10 looks at erotic fiction's place within the traditional publishing industry.

10

Traditional publishing

You've gone to a lot of trouble to produce a good piece of erotic fiction. You're probably keen to send your work out into the world, and you may hope that it finds a paying audience.

There are two routes to getting your work published for money. The first route is traditional publishing, when the writer works with a publishing house. That's the subject of this chapter. The second route, self-publishing, is when the writer goes it alone and takes responsibility for each stage in the publishing process herself. We turn to this in Chapter 11.

Traditional publishing is big business. As businesses, publishing companies must make money. They do this by paying writers for stories, using their expertise to turn the stories into sellable products, then selling the product on to the reading public. It is essential that published books generate sufficient sales to pay for the resources and infrastructure of the publishing house, so traditional publishers are choosy about which writers and stories they take on.

If you hope to pursue the traditional publishing route, either now or when you have more experience as a writer, this chapter will help you to understand this multi-million-pound global industry.

Publishers of erotic fiction

If your wildest dreams in Chapter 2 included seeing your story on the shelves of your favourite bookshop or local supermarket, you'll need to win a contract with one of the larger mainstream publishing companies, with their powerful marketing and distribution networks. In every genre, the competition to land such a contract is intense.

If you're hoping for steady, decent sales to a loyal band of erotic fiction fans, particularly if your work pushes the boundaries of what would be acceptable to the mass market, you may be better off targeting specialist erotic fiction publishers. Writers contracted to specialist publishers may not become household names, but they can enjoy fame and fortune within the erotic fiction community.

Now that you've read widely in the genre and have started to write, it's likely that you have some idea of where your strengths and your interests lie.

MAINSTREAM PUBLISHERS

Mainstream publishers tend to be conservative. To be profitable, their books must appeal to the widest possible market; it makes no commercial sense to take risks and push boundaries. Few mainstream editors would have taken the risk of taking on *Fifty Shades* if it had first landed on their desks. But, across the world, mainstream readers bought it in their millions. The market for erotic fiction was shown to be bigger than previously thought.

Some publishers have responded by setting up new lines dedicated to erotic fiction and erotic romance, such as HarperCollins with their e-book imprint Mischief. Virgin Books (part of the Random House group) revived their ground-breaking Black Lace imprint, which had originally been set up in the 1990s to provide 'erotica for women by women', a market niche that had previously been largely neglected.

Setting aside the *Fifty* phenomenon, there has been a steady eroticization of mainstream fiction over recent years. Romance readers in particular are no longer content to stay on the wrong side of the closed bedroom door. Harlequin Mills & Boon has a venerable history for popular romance, but their Spice line is no-holds-barred erotic fiction, and their Blaze and Nocturne lines are erotic romance.

SPECIALIST EROTIC FICTION PUBLISHERS

With the rise of the Internet, it has never been easier to find and access erotic fiction. And e-reading is the perfect medium for the genre. Whether readers are looking for, buying or enjoying sexy stories, they can keep their guilty pleasures private.

These changes have enabled presses like Xcite Books, Total-E-Bound and Ellora's Cave to grow and become influential in the field. Headed by experts, specialist publishers have more flexibility to explore niches and they can deliver alternative voices and content without upsetting mainstream shareholders. They often have fewer limits and a greater tolerance of transgression. Take a look at Burning Book Press (burningbookpress.com) for an edgy approach to the genre.

The specialists have become trusted sources. This brings readers back for more, especially if the mainstream doesn't deliver what they're looking for. And many writers enjoy the more intimate relationship that comes from working with a smaller specialist publisher. Having cultivated both writers and readers, these specialist publishers have been well placed to profit from recent surges in the market for erotic fiction.

To be successful in a niche, even one as large and lucrative as erotic fiction, overheads must be kept low. This is easier with digital delivery. Therefore, many specialists produce only e-books. Some publishers release print editions once stories have demonstrated commercial appeal.

The benefits of traditional publishing

If you want to make money from your writing and you have the right story to sell, a traditional publisher will invest in your work. These are the benefits of working with a traditional publishing house:

- **A contract.** The contract details your responsibilities and the publisher's rights to sell your work globally. Some mainstream publishers may offer you an advance, money paid to you in anticipation of future sales. E-publishers don't usually offer advances; royalty-only contracts are becoming widespread.

- **An editor.** You will have access to an experienced professional who can offer advice and assistance, helping you to realize the potential of your work.
- **Professional production and design.** Your manuscript will go through a number of stages on its way to becoming a finished product. It will be copyedited then typeset and printed for hard copies, or coded for digital editions. A design professional will produce the cover.
- **Publicity, marketing and sales.** Publishers have staff who can generate media interest and reviews, run social media campaigns, and advertise your work. Branding is important for publishers, and this should work on the writer's behalf; if a company rates highly in web searches for a particular type of title, it is easier to make sales. Sales staff negotiate with retailers such as supermarkets, bookseller chains or independent bookshops, giving you access to a large readership.
- **Warehousing and distribution.** The publisher takes care of logistics, ensuring that your book is in stock and is dispatched to fulfil orders internationally, whatever format it takes.
- **Payment.** You will receive a royalty for each copy of your book that is sold.

Working with a traditional publisher means that someone is keen to invest money and time in your erotic fiction, leaving you free to concentrate on your writing. It's a stamp of approval that's recognized by readers and reviewers.

Three publisher profiles

In the Appendix we've included a selection of erotic fiction publishers. It provides you with a good starting point for finding out more about who's buying and what's selling.

Anyone writing within a genre should know about its more influential players. The following publisher profiles provide a short introduction to three companies that are reputable erotic fiction specialists.

XCITE BOOKS

Hazel Cushion, CEO Xcite Books

'Sex is recession-proof.'

Xcite Books is the UK's largest print publisher of erotic fiction. The women-friendly erotic imprint, launched in 2007, produces fiction in paperback, e-book and audio formats. We discuss their range in 'What publishers want', below.

The company believes its success is built on the talent of its authors and editors, with their expert editorial team working closely with writers to hone accepted stories. The combination of detailed submission guidelines and professional editing ensure that standards are kept high. This is vital – it's essential to the company that that reader trust in the brand is maintained.

Xcite are proactive marketers. Titles have been distributed free with magazines and sold in Ann Summers shops. Hazel Cushion, Xcite founder and CEO, has worked with libraries to develop the Between the Sheets reading campaign, and is keen to point out the health benefits of reading erotic fiction.

Xcite writers are based all over the world, and new writers are welcomed.

TOTAL-E-BOUND

Tina Burns, Editor-in-Chief, Total-E-Bound

'To maintain a dominant position within this ever-changing industry, it is essential to publish quality erotic romance.'

(from www.total-e-bound.com)

With a global customer base, Total-E-Bound is Europe's largest e-book publisher of erotic romance fiction. Founded in 2007 by Claire Siemaszkiewicz, Total-E-Bound offers 'pure unadulterated escapism for today's modern reader' and works with some of the hottest erotic romance authors in the world. The company publishes six titles every week, available in all e-formats. Titles include 'hot historicals, salacious sci-fi, scorching supernatural fiction and … all tastes from boy-meets-girl and boy-meets-boy, to BDSM, threesomes, foursomes and moresomes'.

Novels published by Total-E-Bound range in intensity from very explicit, hot reads to more sensual erotic romance stories and everything in between, including sexy reinterpretations of the classics. New writers are encouraged to submit.

ELLORA'S CAVE

 ## Ellora's Cave website

'We want great storytelling, fresh writing, compelling characters and hot sex that will thrill our readers and capture their imagination.'

(www.ellorascave.com)

In the late 1990s Tina Engler began writing the type of romance novel she wanted to read, with strong, intelligent heroines and detailed sex scenes, using words people really use, not flowery euphemisms. In 2002 she set up what has become a multi-million-dollar publishing empire, selling over 200,000 books a month. Ellora's Cave has over 4,000 titles available for download from e-book retailers and from their own site, and print versions are available on demand. Bestsellers are published in paperback.

They publish a minimum of nine new titles across their imprints each week. Favourite categories are paranormal, fantasy, erotic romance and BDSM. They have around 800 writers, several of whom are award-winning authors in the erotic romance genre.

Ellora's Cave is open to new submissions.

How to find a publisher

When you're ready to submit your work to a publishing house and you've found out about a few that publish work similar to your own, who should you approach? Here's how to decide. For each publisher, answer the following questions under these headings:

1 *Research the types of erotic fiction that they have on their list.*
- Do they publish authors that you enjoy?
- Do they publish categories or themes that interest you as a writer?
- Do they draw a line that you'd rather cross, or cross lines you'd rather not?

2 *Assess the production and promotion standards.*
- Do you like the covers they use and the way they market their titles?
- How easy is their website to navigate, and how appealing is it?
- What formats do they publish in? For example, are you happy with publication in e-book only?
- Where do they sell? If sales are predominantly in the US and you are a UK writer, you need to think about what will and will not work for different cultures. This goes beyond the words you choose and the setting for your story. If you set work in an unfamiliar culture, you risk breaking social conventions without being aware of them.

3 *If it's a relatively new publisher, check their credentials.*
- How are they perceived by other writers and the industry at large? It is relatively easy to set up as an e-publisher. If they are not one of the larger, well-established and reputable companies, you can check them against the 'not recommended' list on the Preditors and Editors website (pred-ed.com), and the list at www.eroticromancepublishers.com.
- How easy it is to order one of their titles?

In the current market, small publishers often come and go. Keep up to date with who's publishing what via sites such as www.erotica-readers.com.

Lucy Felthouse, author

'There are some horrific publishers out there and some horror stories from the poor authors that signed with them. Speak to other authors and ask for opinions and recommendations.'

Identify your target publisher

- Starting with our list in the Appendix, look at different publishers' websites and make a list of those who publish in your sub-genre.
- Identify which publishers you like the look of, and why. For example, you might like the covers, the relationship they have with readers, or the range of categories they carry.
- Who would you really like to publish your work? Once you have a shortlist of three possible publishers, find their submission guidelines.
- Buy at least one of their recent publications in your chosen category. Was this easy to do?
- Identify your primary target.

Do I need an agent?

An agent looks after a novelist's writing life and business affairs. They pitch proposals to publishers and they negotiate on advances and royalty rates. Agents try to get the best deals for different territory and format rights.

Mainstream publishing houses prefer to work with agents as they ensure that only high-quality proposals are submitted. If you are writing at the literary or mass-market end of the spectrum, you should consider finding one.

Publishers who specialize in erotic fiction usually don't require authors to have an agent – the three we profiled earlier in this chapter don't. These publishers also tend to have straightforward contracts that do not require negotiations. Agents usually charge a commission of 10 to 15 per cent, so you need to decide whether it's worth splitting your hard-earned money with them.

Agents are not required for the short-story market.

There are fewer agents who specialize in erotic fiction, so you might approach those who focus on literary fiction or commercial fiction, women's fiction or genre fiction. Look for agents in *The Writers' and Artists' Yearbook* (A & C Black). If agents are open to submissions, their listings will say so and will tell you what to submit. If they are closed, or only take referrals, don't waste your time on the off-chance. A site with a useful list, and good advice about perseverance, is www.literaryrejections.com.

As agents make their money from commission, they can be reluctant to take on a first-time author, even if they really like your writing. An agent will need to believe that she will earn enough to justify representing you. When you approach them, you need to show that you are a credible author who takes their writing ambitions seriously.

What publishers want

Hazel Cushion, CEO Xcite Books

'You need to be professional, show you know what you're doing, follow submission guidelines.'

- More than anything, publishers and readers want good stories that have been written well, meeting their expectations in terms of category and heat. Publishers are looking for content that reflects other successful stories. Most publishers of erotic fiction issue guidelines for writers on their websites.

- Different imprints from the same publisher will have different requirements. If you mix up the requirements of two imprints, you're likely to end up with a story that's suitable for neither. For example, Xcite Books have three specific imprints, and their website makes clear what fits in each. From their website:

  - The Secret Library offers novella-length romances with discreet covers for readers who like strong characterization and a more developed heterosexual relationship, together with explicit, passionate sex.

  - The general Xcite range is aimed at women and couples and offers mainstream short-story anthologies and erotic novels with mixed and varied themes (mild BDSM elements, multiple partners, gay and lesbian).

  - The Xtrm range offers more explicit BDSM and fetish themes – the content is consensual but characters may be pushed beyond their comfort zones. The website provides clear guidelines that edgier scenes can include 'golden showers and breast suckling but no scat, bestiality, incest or non-consensual activity. No extreme violence (i.e. no insertion of weapons such as guns/knives).'

If you want the benefits of working with a traditional publisher, you need to give them exactly what they want.

- Match your heat level to the guidelines given.
- If the editor gives a list of clichés and hackneyed plots they never want to see again, they mean it.
- Some publishers of erotic romance will say whether they want the lead character to be the male or the female.
- Keep to the specified word count.
- If publishers ask to see the final chapter, don't submit before you have one.
- If you see the words 'no unsolicited author material', then don't send your work.

What to send

Apart from being familiar with the work they publish, what else will a publishing company expect from you? Here's what you often have to send when you are making a submission.

- **A manuscript that meets the publisher's guidelines.** If you've submitted to one publisher, don't assume that changing the email address and a few details in the covering letter will be all that's needed before submitting to another publisher. You may have to do another draft, specifically to address heat issues, for example. It's worth having a particular publisher and their specific guidelines in mind when you start to write longer fiction.
- **A manuscript that's clearly laid out.** Again, this may be covered in the guidelines. If not, a good standard is Times New Roman, 12 point, double spaced. If you are asked to submit hard copy manuscripts, only print on one side of the paper. Number pages, and put your name and the story's title in your header. There is no need to place copyright symbols on every page – the publisher is not in the business of stealing your work. Give a word count.

- **For novels and longer novellas, sample chapters rather than the full manuscript.** Sample chapters should be from the start of your novel. Don't be tempted to send chapters that you think are better than your opening chapters. For one thing, the editor needs to see how you introduce and develop the characters and plot. For another, your opening chapters need to be among your best if you want to engage the reader.
- **A synopsis.** This is a brief overview of your longer-form erotic fiction. Publishers may request a particular length of synopsis, or state how it should be set out. There are more details in the section below.
- **If you are proposing a series, some information about the subsequent titles.** Be aware that, from a marketing point of view, it's best to have two or three books ready for staged release after the initial launch.
- **A covering email.** This might include the following:
  - A short description of your work
  - What you've read from their list, and what you have enjoyed. Genuine flattery is appreciated but don't overdo it.
  - Any similarities between your work and one of their existing writers' successful pieces. If you can demonstrate what you know about the market and identify where your title may fit within it, the publisher will see that you are taking your writing seriously. She is more likely to take it seriously, too.
  - Your previous publishing successes. If you are social-media savvy, include links to your Twitter feed or website. If you haven't been published yet, you may briefly mention any writing groups you belong to or classes you've taken, but this should be very brief indeed, with the intention of showing your commitment to writing. Letting the publisher know that you belong to forums or read blogs in the erotic writing community is another way of showing your enthusiasm for the genre. The publisher is not interested in what your best friend or your mum thinks about your writing.
  - How you think they might position and market your work if it is different from the other books on their list. What are its unique selling points? What will it do for the reader?

Finally, when you've collected everything together and made sure that it meets the guidelines (have we said this enough?), email your submission to the correct person, spelling their name properly. That might sound obvious, but it's worth double-checking.

If you are looking for an agent, you may be asked to send a similar submission package.

 ## Victoria Blisse, author

'A good covering letter is polite, to the point and precise. Make sure you add in your name and contact details as well as anything else asked for: a word count of your story, a brief description and a synopsis, too, if it has been requested. Don't be over-friendly – it is a business email or letter, and the tone should reflect that.'

The synopsis

If you are submitting longer fiction, the publisher will read your sample chapters. If she likes what she sees, she will look at your synopsis. The synopsis is a concise summary of your story, often one or two pages long – submission guidelines may state what is required. She'll check that the rest of your story makes good on the promise of those sample chapters: that you know how to handle plot and character development, that you honour the conventions of the sub-genre, and that you meet the requirements of the imprint.

With only a couple of pages to get your story across, it's worth spending some time on getting this right. If the synopsis ticks the publisher's boxes, she may ask to see the rest of your manuscript.

Anyone starting a synopsis from scratch might worry about what to include and what to leave out. However, you have a head start. You'll have created a story outline of your key scenes and linking sections in Chapter 6 when we discussed plot, and a map of your story, showing how the scenes turned out, for structural revision in Chapter 9. You can use these in creating your synopsis.

Summarize each scene in a few sentences. Describe how the scene opens, what the character's goal is, what happens in the scene, and how the scene ends. Give more weight to the key scenes – you can go into more detail with these as they are the important points of the novel.

Include all the main points of your story. Don't try to entice the publisher by holding back the denouement as though you were writing cover blurb, or by keeping the ending close to your chest in case your great idea is stolen. The publisher needs to know that you can deliver right to the end.

Do I need a pen name?

There are many good reasons for writing erotic fiction under a different name.

- You're concerned that your involvement with erotic fiction may have a negative impact on another part of your life, such as your day job.
- You worry that your real name might put readers off. For example, many male erotic fiction writers publish under female pen names.
- You want to keep your erotic fiction identity separate from your other genre identity, to protect your brand.

Pick a pen name

Brainstorm possible pen names. If you're stuck, think of first or second names in your family, names you've always liked, names that would be relevant to any of your leisure activities (keep it clean!) or names of your heroes.

- Try saying each one out loud – can you imagine being called that?
- Are they easy to remember and to pronounce? Bland or difficult names won't help.
- Pick some favourites and search for them online. Are they too similar to other writers' names?
- From a business point of view, can you buy a domain name to match any of them?
- You might need a deadline for this, too. Plan to make a submission soon, and pick your new pen name for sending it out.

Publishers and editors will respect your wishes regarding pen names. Advice from Angela James on the Carina Press blog suggests you need to be comfortable with the name that you pick. It must stand the test of time and sound serious enough to reflect the approach you're taking to your writing. Avoid sounding like a bad porn actor.

Consider pairing your own first name, a shortened version of it, or your own nickname with a different surname – you'll respond when someone addresses you by it, and you won't have to keep track of which name to use when you introduce yourself or sign copies for fans.

Submit

- Go to one of the following websites:
  - www.circlet.com
  - www.littleravenpublishing.com
  - www.total-e-bound.com/submissionguidelines. asp?#current
  - www.mischiefbooks.com/pages/contact
  - www.cliterati.co.uk/erotic-writing-tips
- Identify which of your stories is the closest fit to their submission criteria.
- Revise the story, tweaking it to meet the criteria if you need to.
- Once you have a final version, leave it for at least 24 hours before checking it again for mistakes.
- Make a submission package, as requested by their guidelines. If there is no guidance, include your manuscript and a covering email.
- Check the spelling of the recipient's name and address.
- Press send.

Congratulations! You've taken a big step towards realizing your wildest dreams. Along with thousands of other readers, we're looking forward to seeing your work.

Many writers don't make it this far. But don't stop here while you wait for a response – what's your next action towards your goals?

After submission

Sending your first submission package off is a climax (ours went snail mail and we kissed the envelope). But then you have to wait. Some publishers indicate how long it will take them to make a decision, and you might have to wait longer than that. For short stories, publishers often state that, if you haven't heard from them within so many months of the submission date, you can assume that you've been unsuccessful.

Waiting patiently for a publisher's response is easier said than done, until you get used to it. Our advice is to celebrate the end of one journey – it's out of your hands for now. Begin another journey; write something new.

THE SHARP SLAP OF REJECTION

It's likely that the response from a traditional publisher will be 'no, thanks'. This is only to be expected – not everything can be published this way. It's very competitive.

Don't take the rejection to heart. It's always hardest the first time – we know. Just remember: it's not personal. There may be any number of reasons why a publisher isn't able to take that piece at that particular time. Perhaps you write well, but you've written the wrong book for the time; it may be in a sub-genre or theme that has currently passed its peak. What's currently hot may have been commissioned a couple of years ago, and now the publisher is looking for what will succeed in a couple of years' time. Or it may be that your work is too racy, even though you tried to stick to the guidelines.

If an editor advises you to revise and then resubmit, she has taken the time to engage with your work. She must see something good in it. Of course, you don't have to take their advice. You may want to try the story as it is elsewhere. However, if you get similar feedback from a number of submissions, you would be wise to take it on board.

The website for the HarperCollins Mischief imprint lists their most common reasons for rejecting manuscripts. While this is a specific to one publisher, most of it can be applied universally.

THE YES, YES, YES OF SUCCESS

Given the number of submissions that are rejected, success is all the sweeter when it comes. If a publisher likes your longer fiction, they will offer you a contract.

As a writer, the contract covers what you will deliver and when you will deliver it. It asserts your copyright as author, and the warranties state your assurances that the work is your own and not libellous.

It covers the publisher's exclusive right to sell the writer's work – when and for how long, where (globally, listed by territory), in what format (e.g. print, digital, audio), and the royalty that the writer will be paid resulting from those sales. The writer usually needs to hold all rights to the work – in other words, it hasn't been published anywhere before. This allows the publisher to sell it across the world, in any format. The copyright for the work will remain with the writer.

The royalty is based on the price the book sells for after the seller's discount has been deducted. This varies according to the sales channels used and the countries in which it is sold. Reputable publishers use a standard contract and are in business to partner authors, not to fleece them. If you do have any concerns as a first-time writer, the Society of Authors will review member's contracts to highlight any unusual practice. Even if you are not a member, their website has lots of valuable advice and reports for new writers (www.societyofauthors.net).

Your publisher may expect to have first refusal on your next book.

The publishing process for novels

Writers are typically given six to nine months to finish their novel. Be professional – meet the deadline you've been set.

After you have sent your completed manuscript to your editor, you will receive feedback. This may include detailed suggestions. For example, the editor may request changes to plot or pacing, or may give advice on improving scenes or developing characters. Editors do want to work with you, so be open to ideas. A good relationship with an editor can improve both your work and your experience of the writer's life.

After discussing the editor's suggestions, you may be able to make improvements to your work before it goes into the next stage of the publishing process. When the copyeditor receives the manuscript, they will check spelling and punctuation, sentence structure, consistency and continuity; they will spot it if your lead pulls on a pair of pumps but slips off a pair of heels. The editor or copyeditor will contact you with any corrections and queries.

When the editing and copyediting stages are complete, your title will go into production. Technology has speeded up production cycles. If it is to be an e-book, your document will be converted – it will be coded so that it can be uploaded to digital distributors in the required formats. E-books can be released within weeks of the final version of the manuscript being delivered; Total-E-Bound estimate that e-books take six months from contract to publication. Some publishers can take a finished manuscript through editorial and typesetting to e-pub conversion in two months. Typesetting and printing physical books take longer, particularly if the print run is over 1,000 and slots have to be booked at the printer. Smaller print runs can be produced fairly quickly by short-run digital presses.

Tabitha Rayne, author

'If you feel defensive when anyone comments on your writing then you are not ready for professional editing. My advice – believe that editors and proofreaders are there to make your work better. And they think enough of your writing style to take the time and effort to do so. You don't have to implement all of their suggestions (be confident to say no if you need to), but I think it becomes a team effort, working together to produce something you can all be very proud of. If you are lucky enough to get an editor who uses track changes for you to approve, pay special attention. This is like a master class in house style and grammar. You can learn so much from the process.'

Earnings

HOW MUCH CAN I EXPECT TO EARN FROM A NOVEL?

Print and digital formats generate different royalty payments.

The royalty percentage for print books is between 8 to 12 per cent, and is usually calculated on net receipts rather than on the recommended retail price (RRP). Net receipts are what's left when the seller's discount has been subtracted. The seller's discount is agreed by the publisher's sales team, and can be anything up to 60 per cent for printed books. So, in the UK, for example, a 10-per-cent royalty on an £8.00 paperback, with a seller's discount of 50 per cent, would earn the writer £0.40 pence per copy sold. Similarly, an $8.00 paper book in the US would earn you 40 cents.

Publishers offer around a 40- to 45-per-cent royalty on the cover price for digital releases sold through their own websites or third-party e-tailers. While this is impressive compared with print royalties, the price of e-books is generally much lower than the print edition, especially in this genre. A current 'sweet spot' price for digital novels by new authors is £2.99 (with print counterparts retailing at around £6.99–£7.99). A royalty of 40 per cent on a £2.99 e-book would earn the writer £1.20 per copy. In the US, where the current sweet spot price is $2.99–4.00, a royalty of 40 per cent would bring in between $1.20 and $1.60 per copy.

You need to sell a lot of copies to bring in a sexy income. That said, the market is large and growing. If you get it right, you will be rewarded by your readers. The bestselling and most prolific authors on the bigger e-publishers lists can earn as much as £10,000 / US$15,000 a month from e-book sales. This means they are probably selling over 8,000 copies across a number of titles. Based on sales figures for erotic romance e-publishers large and small, the average number of sales is more likely to be around 300 in the first month, 1,000 in the first year and 2,000 for titles that have been out for more than one year.

As soon as you start earning money from your writing, get advice from an accountant.

HOW MUCH CAN I EXPECT TO EARN FROM SHORT FICTION?

For short stories and anthology entries, you can expect to earn a flat fee from around £25 / US$40 to (less commonly) £100 / $150, depending on word count. Payment is usually made on publication. Print anthologies often offer better rates than their online counterparts. Circlet Press publishes short fiction of 250 to 1,000 words on their website, paying $5 for each via PayPal.

M.K. Elliott, author

'The great thing about a short story is that it has such immediate gratification, both for the writer and the reader. There isn't the six months writing the first draft, followed by another six months of revisions, then another six months of submitting before you even hear something. Writing short stories is fun, and getting the acceptances is even better.'

Erotic shorts also suit the growing mobile readership. Maureen Scott, CEO of Ether Books, a social reading app that publishes stories to smartphones and tablets, urges erotic fiction writers to join the sexting set. Ether Books is more a distributor than publisher. They don't buy the rights to your work in the same way as a traditional publisher does, but you can rent space on their platform and be paid a 20-per-cent royalty for each download. It's a quick way to get published, anonymously if you wish, and you can get feedback from readers and other writers (www.etherbooks.com).

Some print magazines and online e-zines carry short erotic fiction. If they pay at all, magazines usually offer a flat fee. Some magazines give guidelines and a contract; others are more casual. Pay attention to the content of the magazine – always study previous editions before you submit. Examples are Peaches (www.peachesmag.com), which pays $25 for erotic pieces, and For the Girls e-zine (www.forthegirls.com/), which pays $15 per flash fiction piece and $25 for longer short stories. For a detailed listing of publications that accept erotic fiction, consider subscribing to the online writers' resource, Duotrope (https://duotrope.com).

Focus points

The old advice of 'Don't give up the day job' applies to writing erotic fiction as much as to any other genre, whether you are going down the traditional or non-traditional route to publication. Writing for a living is bloody hard work.

Finding the right audience with the right subject matter at the right time is largely down to luck – no one can predict the next E.L. James. But this is a word-of-mouth business. If your story ideas and your writing style ensure that readers come back, and that they recommend you to their friends, you could be one of the lucky ones.

Things to remember

- Traditional publishing companies are businesses that have to make money in a competitive industry. They can't publish everyone.
- Mainstream publishers often have more resources than erotic fiction specialists, but they are more conservative and competition for contracts is fierce.
- Specialist publishers find out what readers of erotic fiction want and supply exactly that.
- Be professional in all your dealings with the publishing industry.
- A synopsis is a selling tool. It's worth spending time to get it right.
- Your work is more likely to be rejected more often than accepted.
- Don't get into erotic fiction just for the money.

Things to do

- Readers demand quality. Aim high to give yourself the best shot at being published.
- Have a target publisher in mind, especially when you are writing longer fiction.
- Find out and follow the submission guidelines for each publisher that you approach.
- In submission packs, send what the publisher asks for – nothing more, nothing less.
- Pick a pen name that you can live with and that doesn't jeopardize your professional image.
- If you become a published author, be a gracious one. Establish good professional relationships with agents, editors, fellow writers and readers, as these can pay dividends.

Where to next?

Given the difficult odds of getting into traditional publishing, many writers decide to take matters into their own hands. We'll be looking at this in detail in the next chapter when we consider how you can get your work out into the marketplace by self-publishing.

11

Self-publishing

The twenty-first century is an exciting time to be a writer. In the last chapter we saw that new technology has allowed niche publishers to spring up, catering for all imaginable erotic tastes. The same technology makes it possible for writers to sell directly to readers and make a profit, even in the smallest niches. The lower costs of digital printing and new e-formats mean that writers can afford to produce their own titles. The Internet has made it possible to sell those titles all around the world.

And self-publishing can be quick. If you sign up to a self-publishing platform, like Kindle Direct Publishing, you could take one of your erotic short stories and release it right now. In a relatively short time, it would be for sale on Amazon for 99p / US$1.50. Job done. But it's probably no surprise that there's a lot more to self-publishing success than that.

So, do you want to print a private library of seductive tales for the lover, or lovers, in your life? Or maybe you hope to supplement your income by releasing a hot alien series as e-books? Or are you tired of trying to catch the traditional publishers' attention? Whatever your reason for considering self-publishing, you need to bring three things to the table if you want a great end result: good writing, lots of enthusiasm and a sensible plan for getting your work out there.

Considering self-publishing

Just as sending submissions to publishers requires a professional approach, so does publishing your own work. Taking on the role of publisher, even for one title, involves all the tasks that the traditional publishing companies perform. They have considerable expertise. There is editing to be done, a cover to design and text to lay out and check. There are digital files to be created or printing to be arranged, and the job of circulating vital data about your book so that it can be marketed, sold and distributed. And that's before we even think about promotion, which we cover in Chapter 12.

Some people say that true self-publishing is when the writer controls every aspect of the process. The more work you do yourself, the less you will have to invest in using other people's expertise, and the more profit you will make. This do-it-all-yourself route may bring you greater satisfaction and financial rewards, but it carries a cost: your time.

Not everyone has the time, or the inclination, to learn to be a publisher as well as learning to write. If you don't, professional publishing expertise can be bought in to help.

However much you decide to handle on your own, be a responsible self-publisher. We don't mean that your stories should carry explicit content warnings, or have condoms on the covers. Readers and retailers are looking for a great reading experience, and they expect a quality product. Aim to supply both.

 ## M.K. Elliott, author

'You need to be a pretty self-sufficient personality as you won't have anyone holding your hand, telling you how wonderful and talented you are, and reassuring you when things don't quite go to plan. When you self-publish, you need to become your own business and learn every aspect.'

The biggest reasons for self-publishing

Why take on the production and sale of your own writing? Many previously traditionally published writers have decided to self-publish some or all of their work.

There are two main reasons:

1 **Money. Publishing is a low-margin business, and yet traditional publishing houses have expensive overheads and must meet a bottom line. As a self-publisher you will keep more of the money, especially with e-formats.**

2 **Creative control. You don't have to wait anxiously for the publisher's 'yes'. You'll be able to go at your own pace, set your own schedules and price, and determine how and where your work will appear.**

If you want to build a successful writing portfolio, being tied to a publisher can be a disadvantage; if any book doesn't perform as well as expected within a given time, you haven't proved your worth. Bigger publishers will be less inclined to keep you on their list or to accept your next book. Poor performance can happen for reasons beyond your control, such as an over-optimistic print run or a competing title. But it can feel as though you've failed. For self-published writers, this is not an issue. They monitor their sales and note when some products work better than others.

In a larger traditional publisher's big pool of writers, you may feel like a little fish. You might think that there's not enough support, and that the publisher is not pushing your work. In a smaller company, where your profile may be higher, the marketing budget and resources are likely to be relatively small. If you're planning to work hard to promote yourself, you might succeed without a publisher taking their cut.

Self-publishing erotic fiction

There are specific benefits in self-publishing erotic fiction compared with other genres:

- Flames, thermometers, heat scales: many readers find these useful but, for writers, they can be restrictive. Self-publishing removes these restrictions. If your content doesn't match what a publisher wants to sell, an editor may insist on changes to your story. We recommend that you listen to professional advice but, if you feel that the integrity of your writing is at stake, you may want to make your own way. This is especially relevant at the edgier end of the genre. Even if you don't want to push the envelope, self-publishing allows for more experimentation with form and sub-genre.

- Self-publishing in e-formats is easier and cheaper to get into than print publishing. Erotic fiction works well on digital platforms and the royalties are higher.

- Erotic fiction is an established genre, and genres have niches, communities and meeting places where readers can easily be found.

- Self-published erotic fiction writers have more control over presentation. You get to choose your own cover. If alpha males with oiled moobs don't do it for you, this is your chance to style the genre.

- There's always the possibility that you may get picked up by a traditional publisher. *Fifty Shades* emerged from the publishing arm of the community site www.thewriterscoffeeshop.com. But be aware that most publishers won't accept your work if it has been offered free of charge, or if it's for sale from your own website or via third parties.

In a blog interview, successful self-publisher M.K. Elliott cites her reasons for deciding to go it alone: the streamlined process makes it quicker to get work out into the marketplace, the revenue is more immediate, the royalty is higher, and writers can analyse the impact of promotion activities to see whether social media campaigns, new covers or pricing strategies are effective. She values the autonomy.

When to resist

There are occasions when you must resist the temptation to get your work out there straight away. This takes self-awareness and honesty.

- **When your writing isn't ready.** We've picked up and rapidly put down self-published titles that were only part cooked. Sigh. If only the authors had consulted an editor or at least sought an independent critique ...

- **When you haven't got the time to do it right.** Even if you outsource most of the tasks, the process takes time, eating into your writing time. And even though you can buy in promotion, no one is going to work as hard to sell your book as you will. Be realistic about how much you can take on.

- **When you skip the research.** If you outsource, you must be sure that you are working with reputable partners. A whole industry has arisen around self-publishing. Some folk will take you for the wrong kind of ride.

- **When you've pushed the boundaries too far.** This is specific to the erotic genre. We hope you have a sense of what is and isn't accepted on mainstream and even specialist sites by now. If you write in taboo areas, such as non-consensual and incest fantasy, you may come under fire. Tread carefully. Erotic writers and publishers have had stories with racy covers or adult content pulled from sales sites.

You are not alone

Thousands of writers have gone before you. Many independent authors are mutually supportive, and there are numerous books, guides and blogs by those who've practised and perfected the art of self-publication. We've included some we've found helpful in the Appendix. Not-for-profit organizations, such as the Alliance of Independent Authors (ALLi) in the UK (www.allianceindependentauthors.org), and the Association of Independent Authors (AIA) in the US (www.independent-authors. org) provide invaluable advice on all aspects of the industry.

Self-publishing self-assessment

Self-publishing needs to be planned well. Assess how ready you are by answering the following questions:

- What can you afford to spend up front? All publishing is based on risk. Can you afford to lose your investment if the gamble for readers doesn't pay off?
- Are you a technical whizz with software? If you're not, how will you plug the skill gap?
- Do you have a good eye for design? If not, this will show. Do you need to employ a designer?
- How do you want to deliver your book to readers? Ideally, it would be available on all digital reading platforms. Can you make this happen, or do you want to keep it simple? Or do you want to hold it in your hand? Having a print edition will cost more, and isn't as easy to sell or distribute.
- How much time do you have to spend producing and promoting? The systems for uploading your work often claim that you can publish in a matter of minutes but, in our experience, it's never that simple. And the most successful self-publishing authors are the ones that get themselves around. Websites, blogs, Twitter, specialist stores – anywhere the erotic community gathers, you need to have a presence.

After all that, if you're still keen, read on.

The self-publishing process

There are a number of processes involved in publishing to sell:
- Editorial and copyediting
- Design and production – internal layout, cover design, proofing, conversion to digital and/or print-ready files
- Uploading of digital files, to distributors, to printers and resellers or readers
- Promotion and sales

Some things have to happen in order, but it is not a wholly linear process. For example, promotion is best begun at an early stage.

EDITING

A conventional publisher will provide advice and feedback on your writing – she'll tell you if your plot needs a twist, or if your favourite word needs weeding out. All writers have blind spots; it's important to seek informed opinions about your work.

Reliable, objective feedback is the first step in quality control. The Erotic Readers & Writers Association (www.erotica-readers.com/) is a good, safe place to discuss your writing. The BookBlogs site (bookblogs.ning.com) features an Erotic Writers Group and Erotic Critique Group where members meet to read, blog, write and publicize books.

While feedback is useful, it's no substitute for careful editing. Even if you've had input from a writing group or sought opinions on an online forum in the early stages, our advice is that you send any novel-length work out to a professional editor. Be prepared to invest in your work; your words are your brand. It can be difficult to find editors and copyeditors who are both willing and experienced in relation to erotic fiction. Consult freelance lists, such as the Society of Editors and Proofreaders Directory Services Directory (www.sfep.org.uk/), or speak to other writers about the editing services they use.

There are three different levels of editing:

1 **A structural edit (also referred to as developmental or substantive editing) looks at your first three chapters or your whole manuscript, assessing its strengths and weaknesses and suggesting improvements to key factors such as plot, pace and character.**

2 **A copyedit corrects spelling, grammar and word usage, and checks that the style is easy to follow. It will pick up errors and inconsistencies.**

3 **Proofreading ensures that your print or digital proof is free from typos or layout errors before the book is printed or the e-book uploaded.**

You can expect to pay around £150 / US$225 for an editorial report on the first three chapters, £350 / US$425 for a full manuscript review and a complete review, and a line-by-line edit of a novel will cost around £500 / US$750 to £600 / US$900. To get an idea of how freelance editors work, take a look at www.thebookanalyst.co.uk and www.winskilleditorial.co.uk.

THE COVER

Everyone judges books by their covers. You'll need to provide a high-resolution image file for yours. Research shows that covers sell books in all formats – they catch the potential reader's eye and pull them in through intrigue, or a promise of what the book is about. But you only have a few seconds to make an impact. What visual story do you want your cover to tell?

Cover inspiration

Put together a mood board of images to reflect one of your own stories. It can include pictures of people to represent your characters, photos of settings, colour swatches, whatever catches your eye.

- Have fun with this. Don't limit yourself when you're gathering material – we have cuttings of buildings, beds, fields, clothing, tattoos, favourite actors, and all manner of random objects that could tell a tale.
- Sign up to Pinterest for inspiring visuals, or browse on Tumblr.
- Are there any stand-out images or aspects of design from the visuals you've collected that might inform your cover art?
- Is there anything in your collection that inspires a whole new story?

Like all aspects of erotic fiction, there are some good covers around and some that are truly awful. By self-publishing, you can choose how your content is packaged. You can be explicit, give an instant signal – feature two women with just a stethoscope between them and you can be pretty sure it's a hot F/F medical tale. At the mainstream retail end, you might expect to communicate your message with more subtlety – perhaps a prop that features in the story (think silk scarf rather than dildo), or an exotic, phallic flower. Clichés, perhaps, but you're looking for a reliable way to let people know what to expect in seconds flat. If you want to move away from the genre stereotypes, to tease the browser or let them fill in the blanks, let the designer get creative. Done well, your cover can still serve to entice or warn, even if you take a fresh approach.

Whatever you choose, the cover must:

- work as a thumbnail – the cover will appear on screen at that size
- be clear, with a legible title and author
- work in black and white for e-readers.

To see what generally works, visit Fixabook for their suggestions about book design (www.fixabook.com).

FORMATS

You want to make it as easy as possible for readers to access your work, whether that's downloading on e-reader, tablet, smartphone or PC, or listening to the audio version on mp3, or buying a physical copy. You should certainly focus on the e-reading options, especially as a new writer. E-books can handle a slow burn, taking their time to find readers. Sales can ignite at any point. Their print counterparts out on the bookshop shelves are stocked on a sale-or-return basis, and are usually sent back to the publisher if they haven't sold in the first few weeks.

If you want to make your e-book available on all digital distribution and sales platforms, you need to have compatible formats. The original file of your edited manuscript must be converted so that the text is 'reflowable'. That is, the text flows on all screen sizes, ensuring that your book looks good whatever the e-reading device. Getting the formatting of your e-book right is as important as checking spelling and punctuation. The most difficult part might be getting your head round all the terminology.

The files you will need to create are:

- **EPUB** – the open standard industry-wide file format used for most e-book readers (Nook, Sony and Kobo), Apple's ibooks, and Aldiko, the e-reader app for Android phones.
- **MOBI** allows your book to be read on Amazon's Kindle and on lots of other devices and e-reading applications. If you have an EPUB file, it can be converted into MOBI.
- **PDF files** can be read by most devices including handheld e-readers and PCs.

If you intend to create the e-book yourself, keep things simple when you're starting out. You will need to mark up your manuscript using HTML codes. If coding isn't your thing, and it isn't ours, there are packages online which you can use for conversion. For example, Calibre is a free open-source e-book application that takes any type of document file, rescales the font sizes and links the book's table of contents to its chapter heads (www.calibre-ebook.com). If you are working on a Mac, export your file directly to EPUB. If you write using authoring software such as Scrivener, your user licence lets you save your manuscript as both EPUB and MOBI files (www.literatureandlatte.com/scrivener.php).

If you're not tech savvy, or you don't have time to get involved with the production nuts and bolts, you can buy in the file formatting and conversion processes. It will cost around £125 / US$200 for a freelancer or e-book conversion service to extract your file, mark it up and then convert it into the different e-reading formats. They will check for device compliancy and layout quality. Get service providers to quote.

Metadata

Metadata is information about your book. It describes your product to the book trade and to other purchasers. Regardless of how you get to the marketplace, good metadata is vital.

The ISBN (International Standard Book Number) is an important piece of metadata. It's the unique identifier for your book. You'll need a different ISBN for each version of your work, such as e-book MOBI, e-book EPUB, or paperback. In the UK, ISBNs are sold by Nielsen, and a minimum of ten must be bought at a time, costing £120. It's Bowker in the US. If you are using a self-publishing service provider, they may supply one of their own ISBNs but, in doing so, they are technically the publisher. Amazon assign their own identifier, so an ISBN is not required if this is your only distributer.

Metadata also includes the title, format, subject category, publisher's name, publication date and availability, cover image, a distributor (e.g. Amazon), the price and territorial rights (where the book can be sold). It must be accurate, as the information will be used by the whole book trade. Other metadata includes a description of the book's content and all the tags, keywords and categories you assign to it. In erotic fiction, the sexier your metadata, the better your sales will be.

The metadata is registered with Nielsen BookData in the UK on an advance information sheet (AI) around six months before your book is released. There's no standard format for the AI – look for examples on the Internet.

E-BOOK DISTRIBUTORS

When you've converted your file into the appropriate formats, you are ready to upload them to major retailers. For Amazon, upload via KDP (Kindle Direct Publishing). For others, such as Apple iBookstore, Barnes & Noble's Nook, Google Play and KOBO, you can upload direct. This will make your title available to the hundreds of thousands of people who buy via these platforms.

But what about all the other places where readers can buy e-books, like Waterstones.com and the mobile phone networks? How can you reach the maximum number of readers out there? In erotic and e-romance fiction, there are specialists retailers such as www. allromanceebooks.com. You can sign up with these boutique e-booksellers as an indie author. Alternatively, use a distribution service to make sure your books get everywhere.

Selling via all the significant e-retailers is easier if you sign up with an e-distributor, also known as an aggregator. Aggregators will upload your title, transmit all the crucial metadata for your book, and simplify the business of reporting sales and managing royalty payments.

One of the first and most successful self-publishing e-book distributors is Smashwords. Run by self-publishing advocate Mark Coker, Smashwords has helped over 50,000 authors publish and sell. Uploading to their site is free and you can convert your Word file using their bespoke Meatgrinder software. Once published, your book is made available in the Smashwords e-store and through all major retailers except Amazon (though you can have the MOBI file you need to upload via KDP). Smashwords distributes to eBook Eros, the largest romance and erotic e-book store (www.ebook-eros.com). The Smashwords website, www.smashwords.com, contains lots of useful free guides that help demystify the self-publishing world.

Using self-publishing services

Partnering up with a do-most-of-it-yourself service provider is one of the most popular ways to self-publish. It enables you to transform your original edited manuscript into the appropriate format and distribute it immediately. You are taken through the formatting step by step and led through the process of creating the metadata. You can set the price and see where your book is selling via the sales reporting tools on your account. You will earn a royalty of up to 70 per cent on each sale. KDP, Nook Press and Kobo Writing Life are all examples of e-book publishers and retailers who operate in this way:

- **KDP** (Kindle Direct Publishing) – register and upload your file to reach readers worldwide on all Kindle devices and free Kindle reading apps.
- **Nook Press** – US book retailing giant Barnes & Noble retailing giant makes the work of self-publishing authors available to all customers with Nook readers.
- **Kobo Writing Life** is the one-stop self-publishing portal for Kobo bookstores (Rakuten) and W.H. Smith in the UK.

If you want a sexy soundtrack and erotic images to pop up in your fiction, then you could consider using Apple's iBooks Author to help you create touch books – but that's another story entirely.

If you want a company to do everything for you, there's been an explosion of businesses offering bespoke self-publishing services. You can choose to buy into a part of the package, or use the complete service as a one-stop shop. Authors Online (www.authorsonline.co.uk/) is an example of a reputable package provider, covering editorial, design and production (e-books and distribution, print on demand and distribution), and marketing. The SilverWood Books website presents various 'publishing pathway' packages and the fees are clearly set out (www.silverwoodbooks. co.uk/). In general, package costs range from a basic service for £500 to a deluxe at £5,000.

If you are choosing to share the workload or delegate completely, put yourself in safe hands. ALLi issues *Choosing a Self-publishing Service*, a regularly updated guide that compares and ranks different providers and tells you what to look out for. Always check the contract and make sure you understand what you're getting for your money.

Do I need to protect my work?

A traditional publisher stands to lose out if they don't pay attention to rights protection. Self-publishers should be aware of this issue. Your words are your intellectual property. In self-publishing, all rights should remain with you.

For e-books, there is a debate in the publishing industry about whether writers should opt to protect their work by applying Digital Rights Management. DRM means digitally locking data so that it cannot be copied.

Some industry gurus believe that easy access to a writer's work is more important than protection against piracy. They say that, when piracy does occur, writers have not seen decreases in their sales. It may be unlikely that someone will go to the trouble of copying your novel, but it does pay to be vigilant.

Erotic fiction is plagiarized most often when it has been posted on the Web for free. It is then lifted and released by someone hoping to make a fast buck.

Self-publishing and print

Despite the rewards of e-publishing, many writers want to hold a print copy of their work in their hands.

Print books cost significantly more to produce than digital files. You may face more challenges selling physical copies of erotic fiction than you would another genre – especially if you're not comfortable whipping out your latest *ménage à trois* in the school playground. Unless your masochistic streak includes pounding the pavements and dealing with raised eyebrows and smothered giggles, be aware that bricks-and-mortar bookstores are reluctant to put self-published titles on their shelves.

DIY PRINT BOOKS

As with e-books, there are a number of options if you want to self-publish in print. You can typeset your own manuscript. It's possible to typeset in Word or Pages, but your finished product will look like a word-processed document rather than a published book. Typesetting is an invisible art, but it adds value, particularly if you want your book to meet professional standards.

If you are going to create the layout yourself using an industry software package, such as Adobe Creative Suite's InDesign, you need to research book design. Consider factors such as legibility and the page extent. Careful attention to font sizes, interline spacing and margins can save you space and therefore money, as well as improving the reading experience.

When your layout is complete, the typeset version must be proofed and corrected. You will then have a print-ready document that can be saved as a PDF file. You are now ready to upload the PDF and your cover file for press.

DIGITAL SHORT RUN AND PRINT ON DEMAND (POD)

It makes economic sense to keep your print run small and use a digital printer. Many print companies offer competitively priced short runs – you can order one copy or 100. If you want a print run of over 800 copies, a traditional offset printer will work out cheaper.

For a short run, try a local company. Get quotes and decide who you'd like to work with. This option is best if you are planning a private circulation, sales through a launch, or other events where you can sell direct. If you plan to sell through all channels, you will have to store, pack, invoice, ship to wherever the customer is, collect their money, and deal with any returns.

If you want to make a print version available through the book trade, consider using a company that can both print and distribute copies. With print on demand (POD), a physical copy of your book is made when a customer places an order. The book can be mailed out within hours. It's an alternative to paying up front for a costly print run which then must be stored. This technology allows some small traditional publishers to offer print formats alongside e-publication.

Your print format must be listed on all the major bookselling sites. The distributors handle order fulfilment in return for a cut of the selling price. You may need to buy into the extra promotions on offer to ensure that your title is proactively pushed to customers.

Amazon's CreateSpace and Lightning Source are both industry POD heavyweights. Lightning Source provides great distribution to booksellers worldwide, but you must register as a publisher with a set of ISBNs. Lulu is the other big player. These companies provide templates for covers and guidelines for book sizes, but you must provide the print-ready files.

You can outsource layout and file preparation to a freelance typesetter. She will work to your brief and produce a print-ready PDF; typesetting costs around £2 / US$3 per page. The final PDF file can then be uploaded to the POD printer.

Printers who serve the traditional book trade also offer a range of services to self-publishing writers. For example, CPi provides a typesetting and printing package (www.cpibooks.com/uk/selfpublishing/). They also offer a distribution and sales package. In addition to providing print copies, CPi will convert your manuscript to the different e-format files for a pence/cents-per-page charge. For an initial set-up fee and a percentage of each unit sold, they will also act as an aggregator for your e-book.

If you have opted to go with a publishing services provider such as Authors Online for your e-book, they should also be able to offer you a print version.

Research the options. When you start networking, ask other writers what worked best for them.

Writing the blurb

If you are printing books, you will need jacket copy. Jacket copy is often referred to as the blurb, and you need this for your e-book, too. You have a few seconds to hook the reader, whether they are browsing in store or online.

- Look closely at the blurb on traditionally published books, both erotic fiction and other genres. Which blurb appeals to you most?
- Using your favourite blurb as a template, rewrite it, inserting details about your own story in place of the original book's details. Does it sound right? If not, try using a different style of blurb as the template. Match the original word count.
- You'll need to describe enough about the characters, setting and plot to intrigue any potential purchasers and make them turn to the first page.
- Think carefully about your book's title. If it isn't strong enough, replace it.

Victoria Blisse, author

'*A catchy title will pull people in to read more of your stories. Don't settle for the first thing you think of. Come up with several options and chose your favourite from there. A good title also needs a good blurb. Start with a short, catchy tagline and then give tantalizing titbits of your plotline. Don't give too much away, but pick out the main points and keep it simple.*'

Costs and returns

As a self-publisher, how much does it cost to get work into the marketplace?

The figures below are a rough guide. We've assumed that your book is 50,000 to 70,000 words long, and that you will undertake most of the work yourself. The extra services we've mentioned above can save you time, but they require upfront investment or lead to reduced royalties. You must decide which services are worth it. If you buy in part or complete packages from a self-publishing service provider, your profits will dwindle. Remember that the profit margin in publishing is small. You could do it all yourself for nothing, but be aware that you're unlikely to end up with a high-quality end product.

E-BOOK COSTS

If you've prepared and converted your manuscript to produce the different format files, either by yourself or using one of the free programs, we recommend investing in editing and proofreading, and cover design. Either way, you'll have to pay for ISBNs.

- Editing can cost from £350 / US$525 up, depending on the level of intervention you require.
- A proofreader for your finished product would cost around £250 / US$325.
- A cover can be produced from £50 / US$75 for a standard template, or up to £750 / US$1,125 for a top designer. Let's say £130 / US$200.
- In the UK, the ISBN you'll need to sell your e-book via international industry-wide systems will set you back £120 (for 10). In the US, single ISBNs cost $125.

This brings the total cost to produce an e-book to £850 / $US 1,175, regardless of how many copies are sold. It would be about £730 / US$1,100 if you use a self-publishing service that supplies you with an ISBN.

PRINT BOOK COSTS

Now, let's look at producing printed copies of the same book:

- You will need to pay for the same elements as in e-book costs, above.
- You will probably pay more for your cover design, as you have to pay for the back cover and spine. Let's say £180 / US$270 (an extra £50 / US$70 or so on top of the e-book).
- You will have to typeset the manuscript. We'll assume that you are doing it yourself. (Otherwise, it would cost £2 / US$3 a page to typeset.)

As a new writer, you probably won't want to risk a large initial print run. With printing, the higher the run, the lower the cost of each copy will be. To achieve economies of scale, you'd have to print thousands of copies. For a small print quantity, use a short-run digital press. If you print one copy of your 50,000- to 70,000-word book, there will be a fixed initial set-up cost of around £50 / US$75. The cost per copy will be between £2 / US$3 to £3 / US$4.50 – let's say £2.50 / US$3.75. There may be a small discount for more copies.

To make and print 200 copies will cost £1,450 / US$2,175. Making this book therefore costs just over £7 / US$10.50 per copy. This is why economies of scale are important in print publishing. Printing only makes economic sense for huge print runs.

The costs of print publishing don't end there. Traditional publishers with larger print runs pay warehousing costs. However, 200 copies will come in five cartons or so, which you may be able to store at home. If you are not using a distributor, you'll need to add in the cost of fulfilling orders. Direct customers will want to click to buy, and you will have to cover the postage and packing costs.

Distribution of print copies has an additional cost. If you want to get your book into the stores, you will need to negotiate discounts. Wholesalers who supply the independent shops and chains will expect you to offer 35 to 55 per cent off the selling price. If you are negotiating with a local shop manager, they may ask for 35 per cent. Chain retailers have central buying departments and it is rare for a self-published title to be taken as a core stock item, even at a discount of 60 per cent.

 ## M.K. Elliott, author

'The introduction and wide acceptance of e-books has meant that authors no longer need to jump through the hoops of agents and publishers to get their work in front of the people who matter the most – the readers. Previously, being self-published meant you'd taken that leap because you couldn't find a publisher who wanted your work. Now authors are turning down publishing contracts in order to put out their work themselves. I am one of those people. I was first published in 2009 by a small press. I had two novels and numerous short stories published by a number of small publishers, but it wasn't until I decided to put out my own collection myself in February 2011 that I actually started to make any money. Now, I am writing full time and earning a living from doing what I love.'

How much can I expect to earn from self-publishing?

Without a doubt, sex sells. You can make money self-publishing, but there's no get-rich-quick scheme. Some lucky and hardworking authors find success and sell enough to earn a good living. For many more, book sales are an additional income stream at best. In the current market, only ten self-published writers a year sell around one million copies. About 150 sell 50,000 copies. The overwhelming majority sell fewer than 300. Whatever the genre, and whatever their route to market, this is the reality for most writers.

Having said that, the amount you receive for each copy sold will be more than if you were traditionally published. Let's look at your e-book. If you price it over US$2.99 on Amazon, you will get a 70-per-cent royalty on the list price (though there are exceptions – read the small print). If you use Smashwords, you will get 85 per cent of net receipts (list price less transaction costs) if you sell on their e-store, and you'll make 60 per cent on the list price for copies sold through other retail distribution partners. If you remember our earlier UK example, our £2.99 traditionally published e-book was going to earn you £1.20 per copy. Self-published, it would make £2.10 per copy. That's a considerable difference to your bottom line.

If you have a print edition and you sell it direct to customers at full list price, you will make considerably more per copy through self-publishing than you would in a traditional publishing scenario. With traditional publishing, you might receive a royalty of 8 to 12 per cent per copy sold. With self-publishing, once you've deducted the costs of manufacture and order fulfilment, you keep the proceeds. However, if you want to distribute widely through the major retailers, including online, you will have to factor in a sales channel percentage cut of between 40 to 60 per cent.

Based on our figures for the traditionally published £8 / US $8 paperback, which would earn you 40 pence / 40 cents per copy, you will still earn more on each book by self-publishing even though you have to cover costs of production and distribution. This might sound good if you make a thousand sales. But traditional publishers have the distribution infrastructure and marketing power to sell hundreds of thousands of copies in print.

Earning reasonable amounts from self-published print is possible only when you're selling lots of books. Unless you have a specific fetish for print, stick with e-formats for your first adventures in the world of erotic fiction self-publishing.

Finally, as mentioned for traditional publishing, you need to account for your earnings. One other thing you do need to consider is the tax situation. For example, you will be taxed automatically on US sales. Make sure you check how to register and claim back this tax when doing your accounts.

Focus points

Self-publishing is now a relatively easy and cheap option. The upside of this is that readers and writers are no longer at the mercy of traditional publishers regarding what can be published and when. The downside is that the self-publishing process can run with no professional publishing input, and this may lead to low-quality products and bad reputations.

Things to remember

- Self-publishing can make commercial sense for erotic fiction.
- Doing it yourself brings creative and financial rewards, but it is hard work.
- Publishing is a low-margin business – pay attention to all costs, royalty rates, sellers' fees and discounts.
- Be professional and maintain the quality of your work at every stage.
- Most erotic fiction writers are not earning a fortune, but some are achieving a good additional income.

Things to do

- As a first-timer, keep it simple and publish an e-book. They're perfect for the genre, and they keep costs down and royalties up.
- Identify the publishing expertise that you need to buy in.
- Do your homework. Research prices, terms and satisfaction levels for self-publishing companies and service providers.
- Work out how much money you are willing to lose before you start spending.
- Think carefully about your title, cover art and blurb – good covers generate sales.

Where to next?

The last two chapters have been about making your erotic fiction available to readers. If you have accurate metadata, some readers will stumble across it as they search for 'erotic' and any other sexy keywords.

But being available for sale isn't the same as selling. If you want to make money, you have to promote your writing. Along with good stories and quality publication, promotion is one of the keys to self-publishing success. Even traditionally published writers are now involved in marketing their work, raising their profiles and building their brand. We'll give you tips and practical exercises for building followers and sales in Chapter 12 – Promotion.

12

Promotion

Bared to You, an erotic novel by Sylvia Day, was a big-budget release. Its promotional campaign included train station adverts and Ann Summers launch events. Even with the significant marketing bill covered by her publisher, Sylvia Day was busy building her brand – just take a look at her website (www.sylviaday.com). *Bared to You* became Penguin's biggest seller for a decade.

Whether you are being published traditionally or you're doing it yourself, you must attract readers. Your fiction may be able to scratch someone's erotic itch, but there's a lot of erotic fiction available. How can you encourage readers to choose your words?

Readers and publishers are attracted to authors who self-promote. If writers already have a platform to build upon, it helps their publishers to publicize the writer's work and increase sales. Self-published writers must learn how to promote their work, because no one else will do it as well as they can. And writers who are self-publishing with the hope of picking up an agent or a publisher still need to generate sales and get their work into the right hands.

As with everything in writing, promotion takes time. If you want more than a private readership, it must be done. In this chapter we look at some of the basic promotion techniques.

Lucy Felthouse, author

'Promotion is hard work, and one of the things many writers like the least about the process. You have to work at getting your name and your books in front of people and also persuade them to buy them. It's a delicate balance between not enough and too much promotion. The whole thing is a fine art and something that constantly evolves.'

So how can you create a burning passion for what you have written? By boosting your profile to increase your audience. To do this:

- Be where readers and writers are.
- Make it easy for them to find you.
- Make it easy for them to talk about you.
- Make them an offer they can't refuse.
- Make the most of third-party assistance.

The amount of marketing and publicity that you can carry out yourself depends on your available time and energy. We know writers who have set themselves punishing schedules and then given up in exhaustion. Remember that you still need time to write. Build a promotion schedule that you can meet.

Be where readers and writers are

Any good marketing plan is based on identifying customers, anticipating their needs, and satisfying them. The erotic fiction genre has its own niche where you can find out how it's done. There are thriving communities and Internet forums, review sites and blog sites where readers will tell anyone who's interested about what they want or don't want in their erotic fiction. You will find people who share your tastes. You'll also find people who don't, but their tastes can be fascinating.

Building an author brand isn't a sinister and insincere form of networking. It's taking part in the conversation about our genre. Discuss what you've read, what you enjoyed, what you didn't, what you think about different styles of erotic writing. You can exchange information and ideas via email lists and message boards, and follow threads of interest. You can subscribe to groups free of charge and move on if it turns out to be not your thing. Being part of the community isn't about collecting data and spamming people with information – it's about joining in and making contact with people who want to engage with your writing.

IN PERSON

It's always great to meet in person, too. Writer Ruby Kiddell founded Eroticon, a conference which brings together people writing creatively and factually about sex. Held in the UK and the US, it is an insightful and inspiring event which hosts speakers, workshops and readings, and supports formal and informal networking (www.writesexright.com). The speakers and the people who attend are friendly, approachable and keen to talk.

Outside special erotic-interest areas online, anyone could be a potential customer. Many readers need only the tiniest encouragement to get talking. When you are socializing or networking offline, there are opportunities to share details of your latest book; have your erotic fiction business cards at the ready. From writing groups to business trips to school fairs, you never know who you might meet. Personal contacts can help spread the word.

The elevator pitch

So, what's your book about? If you meet a publisher, an agent or a reader in a lift, and have only a few seconds to describe your latest book, it helps if you have something coherent to say.

Fill in the blanks, and delete as appropriate:

It's an erotic fiction [novel/novella/short story] about a [woman/ man/alien/other] in [a couple of words to describe the setting] who [brief description of the Inciting Incident], and [she/he/it] [description of the sexual issue] to [the lead's story goal]. It's turned out well – the sex scenes are really hot. Would you like my card? It's got my contact details on it, and you can find out more about [your story's title] on my website.

Practise this!

This is a really useful description to have on the tip of your tongue. We've found that people are eager to listen when you mention the 'e' word; grabbing attention with your first line and describing your fiction succinctly can turn listeners into readers.

Be inventive. If you've decided on a small print run and you like to party, you could hold a raunch launch at a local bookshop, sex shop or library. Or create a buzz by providing a short reading guide and hosting or visiting book groups. While erotic reading is mostly a private affair, we've had great fun reading aloud at social gatherings, and it's a good way of getting feedback and inspiration.

MAGAZINES, COMMUNITY SITES AND FORUMS

There are countless opportunities to get your work out to an unlimited audience via the Internet.

The quality of sites varies widely. They range from expertly curated communities, such as the Erotic Readers & Writers Association (ERWA), to broader adult chat platforms where you can pay-to-view written porn or write personal stories for clients. The idea of private contracts is not new. Anaïs Nin sold her erotic stories to a private collector for a dollar per page.

If you want exposure or feedback rather than payment, there are reputable sites where you can upload your stories for free. This especially suits the short form. Joining and submitting can be a great way to develop your writing skills and market knowledge, and to build relationships. You don't get paid this way; once a finished piece is out there, it can be considered published. This is important if you had hoped to sell it later. Even though the copyright is yours, if you've posted your writing on the Internet, it can be harder to control what happens to it.

At the following sites, you can freely read, publish and, in some cases, sign up for either a 'like' or for deeper, constructive criticism (more in the Appendix):

- **Clean Sheets** (www.cleansheets.com) Literary erotica, fresh each week; 3,000-plus readers a day viewing millions of pages each month. This is a source for Susie Bright and Mammoth Books's Best Erotica series, and stories earn a copy of the anthology in lieu of a fee. Running since 1998.
- **Cliterati** (www.cliterati.co.uk) The UK's original erotica site for women is now open to all. Editor-in-chief Emily Dubberley was

the founder of *Scarlet* magazine and is a leading figure in the British erotic community. Fiction and fantasies are themed as group, kinky, queer or straight. The site carries news, reviews, sex science, education and advice. Running since 2001.

- **Erotic Readers & Writers Association** (www.erotica-readers.com) Includes an email discussion list, newsletter, story gallery, market news and a list of publishers and submissions.
- **Literotica** (literotica.com) Popular writers can get up to 30,000 readers per story. A feedback system is in place.

Writers become valuable members of online sites through posting and message boards. Some sites are good sources for calls for submissions. The ERWA site has a treasure trove of articles from seasoned authors. It provides useful links and resources to encourage and inspire writers interested in erotic fiction and its sub-genres. They offer 'a secure [and free] place to network and discuss the writing process' through their writers' email list.

Founded by Sylvia Day, Passionate Ink is the erotic arm of the Romance Writers of America. Their goal is to promote knowledge and respect for the genre through education about the sub-genres and heat levels, and to provide a platform for writers in the industry.

More general sites, such as Goodread.com, have sections where you can seek suggestions and encouragement.

Another outlet for writing and sharing is through fan fiction communities, such as www.fanfiction.net. On these sites, people who experience a passionate connection with another writer's characters or a fictional world pick up where the story left off, carrying it beyond its original boundaries. Contributors often add erotic content left out by the original writer, or take existing sexual episodes up a notch, or take them in a completely different direction by changing character combinations and sexual flavours. Sometimes contributors export other writers' characters into an alternative fictional universe. If you have a literary obsession, you get to choose the fantasy.

If you want to experiment in this way, find out about the codes of the community first. For example, respect the wishes of writers who don't welcome fan fiction based on their work. Ethical fan fiction contributors do not profit from other writers' imaginations or from fellow community members' suggestions.

There are many benefits of sharing your work. Self-publishers, in particular, are a collaborative bunch. Erotic fiction writers are often mutually supportive, and they co-promote each other's work online. In the section on blogging, below, we suggest sites where you will see this in action.

 ## Victoria Blisse, author

'Make friends with other authors in your genre. You may think that you don't want the attention of authors; you want readers. But don't forget that those authors also read in the genre, too. Even if they don't buy your work, they can help you promote. Maybe they'll re-tweet or share your posts on social media, or you might be able to schedule a guest blog post with them. Some of my biggest and most profitable opportunities have come through from my authorly friends. Their support is invaluable.'

Make it easy for readers to find you

When you are active in the erotic community, readers will get to know your name and they'll want to know where to find your work. In *The Smashwords Book Marketing Guide*, Mark Coker points out ways to make it easy for readers to connect with you, from including a hyperlink to your book when you sign off an email, to preparing a press release and sending it out. With online social media, reading recommendations can spread to hundreds of thousands of users in minutes, but research shows that it can take from six to twelve encounters with a title before readers are ready to purchase. The earlier you start to build momentum and make contact with readers, the stronger the buzz will be.

KEY PLATFORMS

There are three key actions in establishing a sound platform for your work: creating and maintaining a website, blogging, and tweeting.

1 Your website

A writer's dedicated website is the solid foundation of their online presence. It is the hub for promotional activity and provides a shop window.

Keep your website fresh. It can feature:
- Extracts of your work
- Your writing CV
- Useful information or insight shared with those who follow you
- Reviews and press releases
- Links to your other social media accounts
- Book trailer video clips.
- A 'buy now' button to push, or links to where your stories are on sale. (Take advantage of the fact that erotic fiction is unusual in that it's often purchased on impulse to satisfy an immediate desire!)

There are several good hosting sites that are inexpensive and easy to use. As adult content is a sensitive area, you will need to find out what material they accept. Weebly.com and godaddy.com are good starting points. Don't forget to advise visitors about the adult content of your site before they enter. Direct sales from websites are a good way to communicate with customers, but you do have to be a good and prompt supplier.

Check out your favourite writers' websites for ideas for your own – we list a few in the Appendix. There are several different approaches. Look at both erotic fiction and other genre writers. Remember that you are in charge of the aesthetics. Let the site reflect your taste, but make sure that it resonates with the content and category of your writing, with no scary surprises.

2 Your blog

A blog can be an online diary about the writing process, about your hot inspirations, and about erotic fiction that you've enjoyed. It can feature the lives of characters, or sexual adventures and fantasies. Writers post work in progress for feedback, test new series ideas, and ask readers why they read what they read. If you provide interesting, well-written and regular entries, readers will subscribe.

Aim to write at least one new piece a week to keep reader interest. One way to keep readers coming back is by serializing a story; if you don't have to make money from a particular story, this is a great way to share your work. In *The Smashwords Book Marketing Guide*, Mark Coker recommends emailing a favourite writer in your genre with a handful of questions for a Q&A post. That writer will then promote your blog through their own social network.

Write for a blog

- Identify the erotic fiction writers whose work you're most familiar with. Look at their blogs and read their recent entries.
- Consider the way that the blogs are presented and their subject matter. Do the blogs reflect the writer's work?
- What do you like about the blogs? What do you dislike? If you have time to maintain it, set up a blog site (for free) using Blogger, Google or WordPress – but check their guidelines for adult content first.
- Write a blog entry of 300 to 500 words about any aspect of erotic fiction that interests you. If you're stuck for a place to start, post one of your erotic fiction short stories.

If you're planning an intensive campaign, you can arrange a blog tour. This is the online equivalent of a book signing tour at bookshops. Team up with host blogs to cover different aspects and excerpts of your writing every day. You can see guest blogs at work at the Erotica For All website (eroticaforall.co.uk). If you don't want to arrange tours yourself, you can hire expert help.

If you can't commit the time to running your own blog, you can be a guest blogger on other sites. Lots of the communities that we mention in this chapter have affiliated blogs, and many are looking for guest writers or reviewers. This can be your chance to talk about your current obsessions. Whatever you want to say, you can sign off with your contact and publication details. Another alternative to doing it all yourself is to share a blog with other writers. In the Appendix we list a few blogs that we've enjoyed.

Because your words are indexed in the blogosphere, blogging is a great way to maintain an active profile. Your posts will record your thinking and development as a writer. The downside is that it's difficult to remove comments that you regret. As with all social media, be mindful of what you write. Remember that publishers and agents may search for your name one day.

3 Tweeting

Many writers tweet, and their tweets feed into their websites and blogs. If you're not on Twitter already, consider its benefits. **With just 140 characters available, including spaces and punctuation, it's quicker to tweet than blog;** these words in bold are a tweet long. So use them wisely:

- Tell people what you're doing and thinking.
- Tell people what has inspired you.
- Give them a meaningful line from your book.
- Spread some erotic gossip about one of your characters.
- Tell a funny anecdote about a sexual encounter.
- Retweet serious news or trends about sex in society.
- Link to a great new erotic novel you've read by shortening the URL (https://bitly.com).

Make tweeting a habit. Aim for one or two thoughtfully constructed tweets per day. Retweet items that fascinate you. Follow tweeters that you admire and find interesting. Whose thoughts matter to you, in the genre and in general? Don't follow too many, though – it will eat into your time for writing and promotion. Don't ask people to follow you. They'll sign up if they want to.

If someone loves your writing and tweets a recommendation to their 10,000 followers, who knows how many sales could result? But avoid the 'buy my book' repetitive push. It really turns people off and, in our genre, you want to turn them on.

Use Twitter

If you don't have a Twitter account, get one at www.twitter.com and begin. It's free.

If you already have one, consider setting up a second account for your erotic writing persona. It's hard to be all things to all people, so you may need to separate your day job from your writing self. Twitter allows you to build a profile – think about what you want to get across.

Lily Harlem, author

'Social media has to be one of the best ways to promote your new book. However, be careful – you could end up with a friend list made up of other authors, or Twitter followers who are all writers themselves. Other writers are not your target audience. You want to reach out to readers. Goodreads is a place where you can do this directly, or you could set yourself up a blog or a website and attract readers there with sexy snippets from your book, competitions, inside information or (and this works really well) have author friends as guests chatting about their latest piece of erotica. This might sound counter-productive. After all, you want readers to buy your book. But this author friend, especially if she's writing in the same sub-genre, will bring readers with her. They might have read all her books and be looking for their next favourite author to enjoy. It could be you!'

OTHER ONLINE PLATFORMS

Now that you're weaving your online web, consider setting up a Facebook writer's page. Shayla Black, Portia Da Costa, K. D. Grace and Rachel Kramer Bussel have them. See what they're doing to attract readers to their pages.

You could create a visual journal, or a storyboard for your latest story. Try Pinterest.com, and search eros, erotic, erotique, erotismo for inspiration for positions, settings and covers (https://pinterest.com/cliterati). You could also set up a Tumblr account (www.tumblr.com).

SEARCHES AND SEARCH ENGINE OPTIMIZATION (SEO)

Readers search for books online. When we enter an item into Google, the search results come back already ranked. A site that appears near the top of search rankings attracts more visitors; many searchers don't read beyond the first page of results. Your ranking can be improved by search engine optimization (SEO).

Make sure that your metadata is accurate (we discussed this in Chapter 11) and identify the best keywords for your book. It's no coincidence that 'fifty' became a popular keyword in titles, blurbs and content. Hyperlink where you can, enabling 'click though' from one book to the next, and from tweets to your website, to increase your visibility. As more sites link to your site and your social media, your web presence becomes more significant.

Readers won't search for your name until you become a known brand. So how will they look for the content that appears in your book? Someone looking for a story about a threesome might search for 'multiple partner', 'ménage', 'sharing', 'group sex', 'swingers', 'mfm' (threesome with no male-on-male contact) or 'ffm' (threesome with female-on-female contact). Use these keywords. Search 'goodreads mfm' to see keywords in action.

Make it easy for readers to talk about you

Word of mouth, or 'word of mouse' (Kotler, *Principles of Marketing*), is another useful tool in writers' promotion campaigns. It starts when readers recommend books to their social circles. Word of mouse led readers from fan fiction to E.L. James's *Fifty Shades* e-book release. Word of mouth helped launch the paperback. The right story available at the right time can grow a fanbase quickly. News of 'must read' books spreads like wildfire through online social media.

A more traditional way to get readers talking is though reviews. Goodreads.com has 16 million subscribers, so a balanced review on a general social reading site is valuable. Consumer recommendations persuade others to read and, especially in this genre, they sell books. This isn't about friends' gushing praise. Only the very naive are fooled by this, and the community of erotic fiction readers is anything but naive. Positive, genuine and considered opinions create interest. If you write constructive reviews of other books, you may see the favour returned. If you admire a writer in the field, she might be prepared to read your work and give it a valuable endorsement.

The reviewers and bloggers who frequent the genre's online communities can make the difference in your promotion campaign. Check how to submit – many request full publication details, a PDF and a cover. You may have to indicate your heat rating so you're matched to an appropriate reviewer. Heat levels on Risqué Reviews (www.risquereviews.com) range from 'Just a Little Slap and Tickle' to 'Wild as a Naked Game of Twister' to 'Requires a Diagram'. In the third category, both the sex scenes and the storyline may push the boundaries.

Review blogs are a great way to keep up with new releases and hot reads. Many link to other sites. We've included a list of review blogs and sites in the Appendix.

Write a review

Choose an erotic novel or short story that you've read since you started writing erotic fiction.

Write a book review of around 200 words:

- What did you like or dislike about the plot, dialogue, characters, pace and style of writing? Was it believable?
- Did you have a favourite character or scene?
- Are there quotes you could choose to illustrate your view?
- Did you respond physically and emotionally?
- Would you reread it?
- Would you recommend it?

Make them an offer they can't refuse

Readers love deals and free stuff. If you're building relationships, why not help close the deal with a special offer?

Self-published writers have the option of using price as a promotion tool. Consider giving your e-book away for a limited period. If you are downloaded free for a month, you stand a good chance of being recommended and sales will build. Some specialist publishers do this for a week to attract readers to new authors, and it works. Think strategically. What if you gave away a story for free which satisfied readers and encouraged them to buy your full-priced titles? If you have a series, why not offer the first book free or at an introductory price to hook readers in? Or have a special 'bundle' price for someone investing in the whole series?

216

If free books sound too risky, you could price at 99 pence or cents. That's an impulse purchase price that really suits this market. Remember the US$2.99 sweet spot? Be aware of the effect that a lower price will have on your royalty from e-tailers, though. Amazon pay 35 per cent on titles under $2.99, and 70 per cent for books between $2.99 and $9.99.

M.K. Elliott, author

'Pricing books depends on two things; whether you want the book to be a steady income earner, or you want to have a go at getting the book on a bestseller list and selling a lot for its category (though be warned, this won't last!). When Some Love It Hot *was at its peak, it hit #11 on the Amazon bestseller list and sold around 80 copies a night. I don't need to tell you that, even at 99 cents, 80 × 0.35 is a decent sum.'*

Browsing titles and reviews is part of the fun of being a reader; we love discovering new worlds to get lost in. Entice people in with titbits. Try a podcast bedtime reading on soundcloud.com, or give away an extract as a simple PDF. Complimentary copies of print books always go down well, too. What are other writers doing to attract an audience? Be creative. Companies such as Vistaprint often have fliers, T-shirts, badges, mugs and mouse mats on special offer: your sexy quotes could make good freebies and promo tools.

Make the most of third parties to help sell

If you are self-publishing and using a distributor, make the most of the tools they offer. Smashwords (www.smashwords.com) provides an author profile page and a page for each title. You can set this up to offer a free sample of your book, and link it to your own network. At Amazon, set up the 'look inside' and 'sample' functions as well as the author page.

For an additional discount to the reseller, you can opt to be part of a distributor's premium service. This may be worth the investment in terms of additional sales. Smashwords authors, for example, are enrolled in the affiliate programme. This provides additional promotion by allowing third-party bloggers, website operators and Internet marketers to promote Smashwords books through hyperlinks. KDP Select is an Amazon package that will enrol your title in their lending scheme in return for exclusive digital distribution rights. Research the available promotion and sales opportunities before you choose a distributor.

If you're marketing a print book, give the suppliers what they need. Booksellers and wholesalers require an advance information sheet (AI) around six months before your book is released (see 'Metadata' in Chapter 11).

Make sure that distributers list your title as being 'in stock' as soon as your print format is available. For example, if you're not in the Amazon Advantage scheme, customers will have to wait longer for delivery, perhaps up to a couple of weeks. This is no good for an impulse buy.

If you're planning a reading event or launch, work with the organizer or bookshop to drum up support. Collaborate. The success of your book is in everyone's interests.

PAYING FOR PROMOTION

Author services companies offer marketing and promotion campaigns and support. Many self-publishing companies have a range of marketing packages. Authoright is a self-publishing project management company. There are examples of marketing campaigns and promotional tools on their website (www.authoright.com).

Service companies may have accounts with major booksellers and e-tailers but, as we've mentioned, having your book available isn't the same as being actively promoted. Check exactly what will be done on your behalf before you spend any money. No one is as enthusiastic about your book as you are, so work with your marketing and sales partners to get them on your side.

 Victoria Blisse, author

'The best way to sell more books is to write more books. A backlist is a real asset to any author, so don't forget that you need to write, even when you're promoting your current new release.'

Focus points

This chapter rounds off the 'Four Ps' from marketing theory:

- **Product** – the great read you're offering
- **Price** – the balance between attracting customers and making money from your erotic fiction
- **Place** – where and how readers can access your work
- **Promotion** – how you let the world know that your erotic fiction exists

If you want to build a business from your erotic fiction, you need a businesslike focus. Keep these four points in mind when you're planning your writing and its distribution.

Things to remember

- Traditionally and self-published writers promote themselves and their work. Don't overcommit on promotion – you need time to write.
- Be respectful when you use social media, and don't post anything you may later regret.
- Find out about the conventions of fan fiction before you get involved.
- Your promotion campaign should accurately reflect the content of your work.

Things to do

- Find where your target readers hang out online, and find out what they want from erotic fiction.
- Reach out to other erotic fiction writers – they're generally friendly, interested and supportive.
- Learn your elevator pitch.
- Strategically share your work.
- When you use a website, a blog and Twitter to raise your profile, keep it all fresh and up to date.

Finally, remember that erotic fiction can reach the parts that other fiction can't. Readers want to be aroused. So, turn them on and brighten their lives, if only for a wonderful erotic moment.

Appendix

Contributors' websites

Victoria Blisse – www.victoriablisse.co.uk
Hazel Cushion – www.hazel-nuts.co.uk/
M.K. Elliott – www.steamyspice.blogspot.co.uk/
Lucy Felthouse – www.lucyfelthouse.co.uk/
Lily Harlem – lilyharlem.com
Remittance Girl (Madeleine Morris) – www.remittancegirl.com/
Tabitha Rayne – www.aneroticadventure.blogspot.co.uk/

From our reading histories

Bankes, L. *Irresistible* (Piccadilly Press, 2012)
Baker, N. *House of Holes* (Simon & Schuster Ltd, 2012)
Bataille, G. *Story of the Eye* (Penguin Modern Classics, 2001)
Bayer, W. *Punish Me With Kisses* (Crossroads Press, digital edition, 2012)
Blume, J. *Forever* (Macmillan's Children's Books, 3rd edition, 2011)
Carter, A. *The Bloody Chamber and Other Stories* (Vintage Classics, 1995)
Cleland, J. *Fanny Hill* (Penguin, 2007)
Conran, S. *Lace* (Canongate Books Ltd, 2012)
Duras, M. *The Lover* (Harper Perennial Modern Classics, 2010)
Friday, N. *My Secret Garden: Women's Sexual Fantasies* (Quartet, 2001)
Hall, S. *The Beautiful Indifference* (Faber and Faber, 2012)
James, E.L. *Fifty Shades of Grey* (Arrow, 2012)
Jong, E. *Fear of Flying* (Vintage, 1994)
Kemp, J. *Twentysix* (Myriad, 2011)
Krantz, J. *Scruples* (Sphere, 2013)
Lawrence, D.H. *Lady Chatterley's Lover* (Penguin Popular Classics, 2011)
Mayer, S. *Twilight* (Atom, 2007)
Miller, H. *Tropic of Cancer* (Quaint, 2012)
Nin, A. *The Delta of Venus* (Penguin Modern Classics, 2000)
Nin, A. *Little Birds* (Penguin Modern Classics, 2002)

Réage, P. *Story of O* (Corgi, 1976)

Rice, A. (A.N. Roquelaure) *The Claiming of Sleeping Beauty* (Sphere, 2012)

Roche, C. *Wetlands* (Fourth Estate, 2009)

Sacher-Masoch, L. *Venus in Furs* (Dover, 2013)

de Sade, M. *Justine* and *The 120 Days of Sodom* (Arrow, 1990)

Sinclair, E. *Jane Eyre Laid Bare* (Pan, 2012)

Ward, J.R. *Dark Lover*, Black Dagger Brotherhood series (Piatkus, 2005)

Notes on writing in the main sub-genres

EROTIC ROMANCE, OR EROMANCE

• Sex sells. Love sells. Sex and love sell very well and are the biggest selling sector of erotic fiction. Mainstream audience for alpha male heroes who are strong, tough yet flawed, and bold, fresh heroines.

• Closest to the romance genre – all about relationship development, typically the monogamous hero/heroine combo and their sensual and sexual connection.

• Happily Ever After (HEA) that comes from a committed relationship is essential.

• The heat can be turned up or down.

• Slow build of tension and desire, leading to hot, intense sex in believable worlds. The sex fits the story, a credible and natural part of the plot.

• Publisher Ellora's Cave has its own trademark, Romantica®. The imprint is defined as their own 'special blend of erotic romance, featuring a central love story, a happy ending and lots of hot sex described in graphic detail, using the kind of language regular people use'. A less racy version is available through their product line, Blush®.

• Spicing up romance classics is enjoying another revival, with titles such as *Jane Eyre Laid Bare* by Eve Sinclair (Pan) and publisher Total-E-Bound launching the Clandestine Classics series.

CLASSIC OR LITERARY EROTIC FICTION

• Western erotic fiction has a long and contentious history – *Fanny Hill, Memoirs of a Woman of Pleasure* is said to be the first erotic novel to be published in English. Written by John Cleland in 1748, it is one of the most prosecuted books in history.

- End of eighteenth century: infamous writings of the Marquis de Sade who gave his name to sadistic sexual practices. *Justine, or the Misfortunes of Virtue* was published in 1791. The controversial *120 Days of Sodom* remained unpublished until the twentieth century.
- Domination and masochism arrived with Leopold von Sacher-Masoch's *Venus in Furs* in 1869.
- In Victorian England, the genre flourished but quality declined – it was a clandestine business. Anonymity and pseudonyms were common. Publishers flouted the law.
- Twentieth-century classics: *Story of the Eye* (1928) by Georges Bataille, *Tropic of Cancer* (1934) and *Tropic of Capricorn* (1938) by Henry Miller and the *Story of O* (1954) by Pauline Réage.
- 1960: the publication of and trial related to D.H. Lawrence's *Lady Chatterley's Lover* helped to reform obscenity laws in Britain. Similarly: Miller's works in the USA.
- 1970s Britain: a revolution in writing about sex, especially in the rise of women authors. Erica Jong's *Fear of Flying* published in 1973, and Anaïs Nin's *Delta of Venus* and *Little Birds* collections published, originally written in the 1940s.
- 1980s and beyond: *The Lover* by Marguerite Duras (1984) and Angela Carter's erotic reworkings of our myths and fairy tales. Today, writers like Charlotte Roche (*Wetlands*, 2009), Sarah Hall (*The Beautiful Indifference*, 2011), Jonathan Kemp (*Twentysix*, 2011) and Nicholson Baker (*House of Holes*, 2012) publish literary erotic fiction.

BDSM

- Bestselling sub-genre that explores alternative sexual practices.
- Covers range of emotion from fun to full-on power play, range of activities from soft horseplay with a crop, to harder pony play with bridles.
- Classics explore some of the more extreme aspects, e.g. de Sade.
- New readers via E.L James's *Fifty Shades* trilogy. Writers and practitioners of BDSM have criticized James's work for being at best unrealistic and at worst damaging; cable ties are dangerous, and those who engage in BDSM don't need to be cured by romance.
- Has become an all-embracing term for a wide range of behaviours but is as much about trust and losing control as it is about the different sensations of touch and the pleasure/pain threshold.

- If not practising, do your homework. Know your knots and the names of the tools of the trade. Vampire gloves draw blood if you use pressure; a misery stick gives more welts and bruises than a paddle; beeswax candles burn hot. Seek advice. Read sex blogs and memoirs. Safe words and gestures are needed for when your characters play close to the edge. Stick to the code of 'safe, sane and consensual'.

CONTEMPORARY EROTIC FICTION

- Sexual adventures of characters with contemporary lifestyles set in contemporary times.
- Reflect the era – bestselling bonkbusters in the 1980s, Shirley Conran's *Lace*, Jackie Collins and Jilly Cooper, with ambition and shoulder pads.
- Today's readers want sexual adventure that reflects their curiosity in all areas – from global settings and characters from different cultures, to unusual pairings and sexually self-sufficient heroines including auto-eroticism.
- Many titles feature an alpha or beta male (caring and sensual), an interesting location and a feisty heroine who's sexy and fun.
- Heat from sensual to dark.
- No requirement to show a romantic relationship – plot can be HFN (Happy For Now) or HEA free. Ellora's Cave categorizes this as 'sex without strings', and their trademark Exotika® imprint focuses on the heroines' sexual experiences rather than on the development of committed relationships.
- In the Ellora's Cave for Men imprint, men's needs, desires and fantasies are made central to the story.

FANTASY AND PARANORMAL

- Contains the supernatural or the magical, and often involves shape-shifters, vampires, werewolves, ghosts, angels and demons – fantastical characters or humans with paranormal abilities. Set in the past, future, in an alternate reality or the contemporary world.
- Eroticizing traditional fairy tales, fables and myths is popular.
- Writers can build worlds and decide what the boundaries are.
- Urban fantasy – set in a city with troubled and dangerous heroes. (One of our personal addictions has been J.R. Ward's Black Dagger Brotherhood series – hot paranormal urban fantasy at its best.)

Writers you might enjoy

Janine Ashbless – dark paranormal: www.janineashbless.com

Maya Banks – hot highlanders: www.mayabanks.com

Jaid Black – sci-fi, time travel, comedy, contemporary, paranormal: www.jaidblack.com

Shayla Black – A *New York Times* and *USA Today* bestselling author; contemporary, ménage, paranormal, historical: www.shaylablack.com

Victoria Blisse – award-winning raunchy romance across the sub-genres: www.victoriablisse.co.uk

Eden Bradley – award-winner who also writes as Eve Berlin; series, BDSM, contemporary: www.edenbradley.com

Susie Bright – *grande dame* of erotica and editor of The Best American Erotica series: www.susiebright.blogs.com

Elizabeth Coldwell – former Editor of *Forum* and responsible for publishing the first stories by many now well-known erotic authors; her own writing encompasses contemporary, ménage, cougar: www.elizabethcoldwell.wordpress.com

Rachel Kramer Bussel – author and prolific anthology editor: www.rachelkramerbussel.com

Portia Da Costa – A *Sunday Times* bestselling author; contemporary, romance, historical, paranormal: www.portiadacosta.com

Lauren Dane – A *New York Times* and *USA Today* bestselling author; contemporary, eromance, paranormal, sci-fi/future/urban fantasy: www.laurendane.com

Sylvia Day – award-winning international bestseller – also writes in other sub-genres under pseudonyms: www.sylviaday.com

M.K. Elliott – themed anthologies, paranormal: www.steamyspice.blogspot.co.uk

Lucy Felthouse – contemporary, eromance:www.lucyfelthouse.co.uk

K. D. Grace: www.kdgrace.co.uk

Lily Harlem – contemporary: www.lilyharlem.com

Megan Hart – erotic romance: www.meganhart.com

Maxim Jakubowski – author and prolific anthology editor: www.maximjakubowski.co.uk

Lorelei James – contemporary Wild West: www.loreleijames.com

Beth Kery – bestseller of eromance: www.bethkery.com

Olivia Knight – www.oliviaknight.co.uk

Kristina Lloyd – Black Lace author: www.kristinalloyd.wordpress.com

Nikki Magennis – Black Lace author: www.nikkimagennis.com

Sadie Matthews – After Dark series: www.hodder.co.uk/Authors
Madeline Moore – 'best oral sex scene' winner:
    www.moremadeline moore.blogspot.co.uk
Tabitha Rayne – eromance, fantasy:
    www.aneroticadventure.blogspot.co.uk
Tiffany Reisz – Original Sinners series: www.tiffanyreisz.com
Remittance Girl – manifesto, opinions and stories:
    www.remittancegirl.com
C.J. Roberts – dark erotica; Dark Duet series: www.aboutcjroberts.com
Mitzi Szereto – author and anthology editor: www.mitziszereto.com
Cecilia Tan – sci fi and fantasy: www.blog.ceciliatan.com
Alison Tyler – prolific erotic fiction editor, BDSM among other themes
    (bisexuality/group): www.alisontyler.com
Saskia Walker – contemporary erotic romance:
    www.saskiawalker.com
James Wood – bondage: jameswooderotica.com
Kristina Wright – prolific in short fiction and editing anthologies:
    www.kristinawright.com

Anthologies

There are collections to suit every interest and taste:
'Best' series of anthologies by Cleis Press; includes annuals such
    as *Best Women's Erotica, Best Erotic Romance, Best Gay
    Romance, Best Bondage:* www.cleispress.com
Dubberley, E. and Fixter, A. *Ultimate Burlesque* (Xcite Books,
    2013). All profits to Macmillan Cancer Support.
Jakubowski, M. (ed.) *The Mammoth Book of Best New* … a series
    of erotica tiles covering international, short stories (Constable &
    Robinson: www.constablerobinson.com)
Jacubowski, M. (ed.) *Sex in the City* series (Xcite Books, 2010)
Kramer Bussel, R. (ed.) Do *Not Disturb: Hotel Sex Stories* (Cleis
    Press, 2009)
Kiddell, R., Weaver, A., Moore, R. and Bailey, W. *Fever: An
    Anthology of Micro-Erotica* (Burning Book Press, 2012)
Perry, R. (ed.) *I Kissed a Girl* (Black Lace, 2012)
Remittance Girl, (ed.) A *Slip of the Lip: ERWA Collection of Kisses*
    (ERWA-RG Publishing, 2009)
Szereto, M. (ed.) *In Sleeping Beauty's Bed* (Cleis Press, 2009)
Szereto, M. (ed.) *Red Velvet & Absinthe: Paranormal Erotic
    Romance* (Cleis Press, 2011)

Szereto, M. (ed.). Th*rones of Desire: Erotic Tales of Swords, Mist and Fire* (Cleis Press, 2012)

Tan, C., and Zaiatz, B. (eds) *Best Erotic Fantasy & Science Fiction, and Fantastic Erotica: The Best of Circlet Press, 2008–2012* (Circlet Press, 2013)

Tyler, A. *Alison's Wonderland* (Mills & Boon Spice, 2010)

Other resources

www.amazon.com/Best-Sellers-Kindle-Store-Erotica/zgbs/digital-text/157057011 the Kindle Best Sellers Erotica list, a useful address for you to keep your eye on as reader–writer

Faulk, M. *How to Find Paid and Free Erotica, Erotic eBooks and Sex Stories* (free Kindle edition, 2013). A guide to finding what you want to read, and what you may want to write. She explains how to search, find free erotic e-books and discover key authors. Includes a glossary of key terms and their alternatives – from age play to bareback, gender transformation to sissification, lactation to pseudo incest.

Wendell, S. and Tan, C. *Beyond Heaving Bosoms: The Smart Bitches' Guide to Romantic Novels* (Simon & Schuster, 2009)

www.passionateink.com: Romance Writers of America erotic fiction group

www.rna-uk.org/ Romantic Novelists' Association, UK, founded 1960

www.feministpornguide.com

www.pornresearch.org

www.wecantgobackwards.org.uk:xeS, sex campaign

Background reading on becoming a writer

Cameron, J. *The Artist's Way: A Course in Discovering and Recovering Your Creative Self* (7th edition, Pan, 2011)

Glei, J.K. *Manage Your Day-to-Day: Build Your Routine, Find Your Focus, and Sharpen Your Creative Mind* (The 99U Book Series, Amazon Publishing, 2013)

Belsky, S., *Making Ideas Happen: Overcoming Obstacles between Vision and Reality* (Penguin Books, 2010)

Blogs, books and websites for research

Belle de Jour. *The Intimate Adventures of a London Call Girl* (Phoenix, 2007)

Coldwell, E. (ed.) *Kama Xcitra: A Sexual Position Guide with 3D Hologram Technology* (Xcite Books, 2013)

Comfort, A. *The Joy of Sex* (Mitchell Beazley, 2011)

Erotic Readers & Writers Association – curated site: www.erotica-readers.com

www.dirtylittlewhispers.com – a lively sex blog from the UK

Dubberley, E. *The Field Guide to F*cking* (Quiver, 2012): www.dubberley.com

Dubberley, M. *Garden of Desires: The Evolution of Women's Sexual Fantasies* (Black Lace, 2013)

www.irregularvoice.com: 'No woman gets an orgasm from shining the kitchen floor.'

www.janesguide.com: comments on sex-related websites

Lee, A. *Girl with a One-track Mind* (Pan, 2010)

Love, B. *The Encyclopaedia of Unusual Sex Practices* (Abacus, 2002)

Gallop, C. *Make Love Not Porn: Technology's Hardcore Impact on Human Behavior* (Kindle edition, TED Books, 2011)

www.makelovenotporn.com – real sex videos from contributors

Szereto, M. (ed.) The *New Black Lace Book of Women's Sexual Fantasies* (Black Lace, 2008)

Millet, C. *The Sexual Life of Catherine M.* (Corgi, 2003)

Violet Blue – sex pundit, educator, agitator: www.tinynibbles.com

Violet Blue, *Ultimate Guides ... to Cunnilingus, Fellatio* (Cleis Press, 2010)

Events and shopping

www.annsummerspartiesuk.com

www.coco-de-mer.com

www.erotica-uk.com/erotica-show

www.traceycox.com (also manuals and how-to guides)

www.volupte-lounge.com

General writing resources

It was difficult to separate out these resource books into different chapters, as they all have much to say about many aspects of writing. These are the books that we turn to time after time. All are highly recommended.

Browne, R. and King, D. *Self-editing for Fiction Writers* (2nd edition, HarperCollins, 2004). Clearly written, and worth reading before you get to the revision stage.

Maas, D. *Writing the Breakout Novel* (Writer's Digest Books, 2001). Excellent on storytelling and covering all the major elements of fiction.

Marks, D. *Inside Story: the Power of the Transformational Arc* (A&C Black, 2009). Uses theme as the basis of plot and character. Ties character transformation to plot development.

McKee, R. *Story: Substance, Structure and Style and the Principles of Screenwriting* (Methuen, 1999). Aimed at the film industry but applicable to all storytelling arts. Excellent on structure and the scene. A challenging read in places.

Schmidt, V.L. *45 Master Characters: Mythic Models for Creating Original Characters* (Writer's Digest Books, 2001). Archetypal characters and plots.

Strunk, Jr., W. and White, E.B. *The Elements of Style* (4th edition, Longman, 1999)

Swain, D.V. *Techniques of the Selling Writer* (University of Oklahoma Press, 1981). If you only read one book about writing, read this. Clear, comprehensive and concise advice and analysis on writing well. Look out for the Motivation Reaction Unit. However, it was first published in 1965 – Swain's style, some of his examples and his vocabulary are now showing their age.

Vogler, C. *The Writer's Journey: Mythic Structure for Writers* (3rd edition, Michael Wise Productions, 2007). Storytelling, plot and character development using the structure of the Hero's Journey, based on Joseph Campbell's ground-breaking analysis of story.

Resources for writing about sex

Morris, D. *Intimate Behaviour* (Jonathan Cape, 1971). Information in Chapter 8 on the 12 stages of increasing sexual intimacy is

taken from Chapter 3 of Morris's book, 'Sexual Intimacy',
pp. 72–102. We use Morris's name for each stage.

Remittance Girl, *A Quiet Revolution*:
   remittancegirl.com/erotic-flash-fiction/a-quiet-revolution/

Knight, A. *Passionate Ink: A Guide to Writing Erotic Romance*
   (Loose Id, 2007)

Lister, A. *How to Write Erotic Fiction and Sex Scenes* (How To
   Books, 2013)

Literary Review's annual Bad Sex in Fiction Award:
   www.literaryreview.co.uk www.huffingtonpost.com/2012/12/04/
   bad-sex-award-2012-infrared_n_2240240.html

Moorcroft, S. *Love Writing: How to Make Money Writing
   Romantic or Erotic Fiction* (Accent Press, 2010)

Publishers – the big trade houses

Avon Red (erotic/romance part of HarperCollins, USA):
   www.avonromance.com

Black Lace (Virgin Books, Ebury/Random House UK):
   www.blacklace.co.uk

Harlequin, including Carina Press (Harlequin's digital-first imprint);
   Harlequin Blaze/Spice/MIRA ('sensual books about sex and
   the modern woman') and Harlequin UK, Mills & Boon Blaze/
   Spice: www.millsandboon.co.uk/books/erotica.htm (Strictly
   speaking, the Canada-based Harlequin is independent, but it is a
   giant.)

Hodder & Stoughton (part of Hachette, UK): www.hodder.co.uk

Mischief (imprint of HarperCollins, UK): www.mischiefbooks.com

Penguin (home to Sylvia Day in the UK): www.penguin.co.uk

Penguin (Berkley Heat/Sensations; New American Library Heat,
   USA): www.us.penguingroup.com

Specialist and independent publishers

Black Velvet Seductions (erotic/romantic):
   www.blackvelvetseductions.com

Breathless Press (erotic romance): www.breathlesspress.com

Burning Book Press (indie e-publisher):
www.burningbookpress.com
Changling Press (erotic adventures, US): www.changelingpress.com
Circlet Press (erotic science fiction, fantasy, and futurism, US):
www.circlet.com
Cleis Press (largest independent queer publishing company in the
US): www.cleispress.com
Coming Together (non-profit/charity erotica):
www.eroticanthology.com
Dreamspinner Press (gay, M/M): www.dreamspinnerpress.com
Go Deeper Press (US): www.godeeperpress.com
Ellora's Cave (trademarked imprints and series, US):
www.ellorascave.com
Erotic Review Books (UK): www.erbooks.com
Excessica (set up by million-seller Selena Kitt – includes taboo areas,
US): www.excessica.com and www.excessica.com/eden
House of Erotica (UK): www.houseoferoticabooks.com
Kensington (Brava and Aphrodisia (hotter), US):
www.kensingtonbooks.com
Loose Id (all sub-genres and themes, US): www.loose-id.com
Mammoth anthologies, UK (Constable, UK and Running Press, US):
www.constablerobinson.com
Oleander Press (Wildheart list, UK): www.oleanderpress.com
Omnific ('Romance without rules'): www.omnificpublishing.com
1001 Nights Press (US): www.1001nightspress.com/#!/page_About
Phaze Books (women's romance and erotic romance): www.phaze.com
Pink Flamingo Publications (BDSM/spanking): www.pinkflamingo.com
Ravenous Romance (all areas, advance of $200 novels/$10 shorts):
www.ravenousromance.com
Red Sage Secrets (erotic/romance, US): www.redsagepub.com
Riptide Publishing (LGBTQ): www.riptidepublishing.com/about
Samhain (eromance, US): www.samhainpublishing.com
Siren (erotic/romance, USA): www.sirenpublishing.com
Torrid Books (US): www.whiskeycreekpress.com/torrid
Total-E-Bound Publishing (UK): www.total-e-bound.com
Velvet Books (new start-up at time of going to press, UK):
www.velvet-books.com
The Writer's Coffee Shop Publishing House (Australia, original, light
erotica): www.ph.thewriterscoffeeshop.com
Xcite Books (erotic romance, UK): www.xcitebooks.co.uk

Other paid outlets

www.etherbooks.com: mobile social reading platform
www.forthegirls.com: erotica ezine
www.peachesmag.com: ezine

Other useful publishing resources

www.aaronline.org (Association of Author's Representatives, US)

www.erotica-readers.com (Erotic Readers & Writers Association (ERWA) – how-to articles, reviews, chat room, up-to-date market lists of anthologies, magazines and publishers)

www.eroticromancepublishers.com (for lists of publishers in the genre (and warnings))

www.duotrope.com (subscription based award-winning writers' resource of where to submit)

www.passionateink.org (erotic romance chapter of Romance Writers of America (RWA))

www.passionatepen.com/romancepubs.htm (for lists of publishers in the genre)

www.pred-ed.com (Preditors and Editors, advice on publishing companies and practices)

www.publishersmarketplace.com (US source of agent, publisher and freelance professionals lists)

www.publishersweekly.com/

www.societyofauthors.net (especially their Quick Guide to Copyright and Moral Rights)

www.writersmarket.com (industry news and advice on publishing and getting paid)

Blake, C. *From Pitch to Publication: Everything You Need to Know to Get Your Novel Published* (Macmillan, 1999)

Bingham, H. *The Writers' and Artists' Yearbook Guide to Getting Published* (A&C Black, 2010)

Writers' & Artists' Yearbook (A&C Black) – a general annual guide featuring lists of agents and publishers, along with full details on how to make submissions. www.writersandartists.co.uk

Self-publishing

Association of Independent Authors, *Self-Publishing! Publish Your Book and Avoid the Pitfalls with Advice from Leading Experts and Experienced Authors* [Kindle Edition, 2012]

Baverstock, A. *The Naked Author – A Guide to Self-publishing*
(A&C Black, 2011) – includes a chapter by Judith

Konrath, J.A. *The Newbie's Guide to Publishing* (Kindle Edition,
2010) http://jakonrath.blogspot.co.uk

Peppitt, E. *How to Self-Publish: A Guardian Masterclass* (Guardian
Books, 2012)

www.publishingtalk.eu/

Ross, O. *Choosing a Self-Publishing Service* (The Alliance of
Independent Authors (ALLi) Guide, 2013)

www.selfpublishingmagazine.co.uk (currently published four times a
year; free article library)

Organizations for indie authors

www.allianceindependentauthors.org
www.independent-authors.org

Feedback and editing

www.autocrit.com (instant editor)
www.thebookanalyst.co.uk (literary consultancy, editing services)
bookblogs.ning.com/group/eroticwritersgroup (feedback group)
www.erotica-readers.com (story gallery)
www.literatureandlatte.com/scrivener.php (content-generation tool
for writers)
www.sfep.org.uk (Society for Editors and Proofreaders Services
Directory – website has lots of useful information about editorial
services)
Truss, L. *Eats, Shoots and Leaves* (Fourth Estate, 2009)
www.winskilleditorial.co.uk (literary consultancy, editing services)

Design, production and distribution

www.authorsonline.co.uk (self-publishing services)
www.bowker.com (ISBNs, US)
www.selfpublishedauthor.com
www.calibre-ebook.com (free DIY e-book conversion program)
www.cpibooks.com/uk/selfpublishing (short run, conversion and
distribution)
www.createspace.com (Amazon, print publishing platform)
www.firstywork.com (e-book conversion services)
www.fixabook.com (cover discussions)

www.kdp.amazon.com/self-publishing (Kindle Direct Publishing, Amazon)

www.kobo.com/writinglife (self-publishing platform)

www.lightningsource.com (short run, POD and distribution)

www.lulu.com (self-publishing platform)

Lupton, E. *Indie Publishing: How to Design and Produce Your Own Book* (Princeton Architectural Press, 2008)

Nielsen: www.isbn.nielsenbook.co.uk (ISBNs, UK; bibliographic data service)

www.nookpress.com (Barnes & Noble self-publishing platform)

www.smashwords.com (Marl Coker – self-publishing guru and e-distributor)

www.silverwoodbooks.co.uk (self-publishing services)

www.unrulyguides.com (links to conversion software)

Promotion

Coker, M. *The Smashwords Book Marketing Guide* (www.smashwords.com, 2012)

Kotler, P., Armstrong, G. and Saunders, J. *Principles of Marketing* (6th edition, Pearson 2013)

Magazines, community sites and forums

Clean Sheets: www.cleansheets.com ('literary erotica, fresh weekly'; 3,000+ readers a day)

Cliterati: www.cliterati.co.uk (UK's original erotica site for women is now open to all; Editor in Chief, Emily Dubberley, founder of *Scarlet* magazine)

Cliterature: www.cliteraturejournal.com (poetry, short stories, novel excerpts, critical works, and artwork; themed quarterly; since 2006)

Erotica For All: www.eroticaforall.co.uk (newsletter, free reads, competitions, guest blogs, call for submissions)

Erotic Readers & Writer's Association: www.erotica-readers.com (email discussion list, newsletter, story gallery, market news, list of publishers and submissions)

Erotic Review: www.eroticreviewmagazine.com ('Highbrow, sexy, funny and controversial – elastic definition of erotic'; since 1995)

Erotic Scribes: www.eroticscribes.com/ (sex news, articles and stories; sponsored by Shhh.com)

EXcessica: www.excessica.com (reader forum discussions, free reads)

FeatherLit www.featherlit.com/the-lovebird-issue (online e-zine edited by Nicki Magennis)

JADE International Erotic Art and Literature magazine accepts contributions on all (legal) aspects of erotica and sexuality: www.greatnorthernpublishing.co.uk/jade.html

Literotica: www.literotica.com (popular writers can get up to 30,000 readers per story; feedback system)

Little Raven Publishing: www.littleravenpublishing.com (blog site which publishes an anthology)

Passionate Ink: www.passionateink.org (message boards, blogs, events, Passionate Plume competitions/awards)

Short Fiction: www.short-fiction.co.uk ('showcase for writing if you don't have technical know-how'; feedback system).

Review blogs and sites

www.ashleylister.co.uk (reviewer and writer)

Black Raven's Reviews: www.blackravensreviews.com

Cliterati, Cliterature Editor, Lucy Felthhouse: www.cliterati.co.uk/subject/erotica/book-extracts/; www.cliterati.co.uk/subject/cliterati-magazine/reviews/books/

Coffee Time Romance: www.coffeetimeromance.com/

Close Encounters with the Night Kind: www.closeencounterswiththenightkind.blogspot.co.uk/

Day Dreaming Book Reviews: www.daydrmzzz.blogspot.co.uk/

Erotica Everyday: www.eroticaeveryday.com/

Erotic Notebook www.eroticnotebook.co.uk/
    Ruby Kiddell: www.writesexright.com

The Erotic Reader www.theeroticreader.com

Erotic Readers & Writers Association: www.erotica-readers.com

Erotica Revealed: www.eroticarevealed.com (D.L.King, Ashley Lister, Alison Tyler)

Erotica Romance Writers (www.eroticaromancewriters.com/

www.eroticwriter.wordpress.com/on-erotica (example of group blogging)

Everything Erotica: www.rtbookreviews.com/genre/erotica (*Romantic Times*)

Fiction Vixen: www.fictionvixen.com (picks of the year and guest
  reviews)
Guilty Pleasures: www.guiltypleasuresbookreviews.com
Just Erotic Romance: www.justeroticromancereviews.com
Kinky Book Reviews: www.kinkybookreviews.com (looking for
  reviewers)
www.lucyfelthouse.co.uk (also organizes blog tours)
Ms. Romantic Reads: www.msromanticreads.wordpress.com
Rainbow Book Reviews: www.rainbow-reviews.com/ (GLBTQ)
Remittance Girl: www.remittancegirl.com/ great links and blog
Risqué Reviews: www.risquereviews.com
Scorching Book Reviews: www.scorchingbookreviews.blogspot.co.uk
www.sevensexyscribes.blogspot.co.uk (example of group blogging)
Smart Bitches Trashy Books: www.smartbitchestrashybooks.com
www.steamyspice.blogspot.co.uk (an example of good practice –
  talks about self-publishing experience, why short stories are
  satisfying to read and write)
Kinky in Ink: www.kinkyinink.com/submissions
WTRAFSOG www.facebook.com
  (WhatToReadAfter50ShadesOfGrey page set up by author
  Summer Daniels, who invited other erotic fiction writers to
  submit their books. It gathered 54,000 likes in a year, including
  thousands of brand-new erotic fiction fans looking for a new fix.)

Specialist retailers

www.allromanceebooks.com (bookseller)
www.ebook-eros.com ('burlesque for the brain' large erotic &
  romance e-books store)

Marketing and promotion resources

www.authoright.com (self-publishing project managers specializing
  in marketing packages)
Baverstock, A. *Marketing Your Book: An Author's Guide* (2nd
  edition, A&C Black, 2007)
Reed, J. *Get Up to Speed with Online Marketing* (Financial Times/
  Prentice Hall, 2010)
Young, D. *Sell Your Books! A Book Promotion Handbook for the
  Self-published or Indie Author* (Silverwood Books, 2012)

Index